ESCAPING THE MAZE

The Redemption of American Management

BY
KENNETH DURHAM & BRUCE KENNEDY

HOUSTON

Quantum Institute
7135 West Tidwell, Suite 119
Houston, TX 77092

The Quantum Institute is a division of Quality International, L.L.P.

Printed in the United States of America

Printing number
2 3 4 5 6 7 8 9 10

Library of Congress Catalog Card Number 95-71685

ISBN 0-9649261-0-5 22.95

Contents

1

Chapter One

The Game

You've probably read about popular business fads failing—TQM, empowerment, ISO 9000, reengineering or any one of a half dozen other prominent programs. Maybe you've heard about the company that won a national quality award but filed for bankruptcy a few years later. Perhaps you yourself have just suffered through another program, complete with speeches, slogans, teams, and new but obscure language, only to see it sputter to a quiet stop on some abandoned road like so many before it. Yet even in the midst of countless examples of failure, the business press still spins stories of success and triumph revolving around these very same initiatives. These inspiring fables usually include CEOs pulling their companies from the brink of disaster. Suddenly, these people become the newest business heroes and their programs the latest business fad.

In spite of the occasional and over-exposed success story, the vast majority of business fads fizzle. Sixty to eighty percent report failure, depending on the improvement program involved and the study quoted[1]. How is it then that New (Business) Wave gurus still find followers? What are the rules of the game? Is this a game worth playing, or should you look elsewhere for help in running your department or company? What separates success from failure? This book provides answers to these and other questions, but not in the traditional sense. We won't tell you how to select the right program. We won't tell you how to avoid the obvious rip-offs. Nonetheless, the answers you'll get will be practical and unequivocal. They will affect the way you look at your company, American business, and the business challenges of the day.

While business fads are not in themselves responsible for the dismal state of American management, they are symptomatic of the general depreciation of general management skills and therefore provide a good jumping off point on our quest for redemption.

BUSINESS FADS, BASEBALL, AND MONOPOLY

The Business Fad Game is similar to any other game. To play it well you have to have a thorough understanding of its foundations. For instance, baseball depends on three premises: (1) good pitching dominates good hitting, (2) a sane person fears an inside fastball, and (3) there is something very Zen about the ninety feet between bases. The good-pitching fundamental has been proven over the long history of the game. Whenever pitching talent wanes, the game degenerates into a slugfest—an ugly form of the game attractive to some fans but distasteful to baseball purists. Baseball fans always pray for a new crop of good pitchers to keep the game in balance. The next fundamental, the fear of the inside fastball, reinforces the good-pitching fundamental. Our natural tendency to pull away from an object heading toward us at 90 miles per hour, coupled with a pitcher's skill to place it within inches of our elbow or head, helps the two fundamentals work together. The last fundamental, the Zen of 90 feet between bases, ensures that the few times we do make contact with the ball, we most likely make it to first base a half-step after the ball does. It so happens that 90 feet also seems to be the perfect distance to the next base, keeping us from advancing between the time the pitcher is committed to a pitch and the catcher can deliver it to second. All three fundamentals are necessary for the game to be simultaneously dynamic during the game and stable over the years.

If you play any well-crafted American game for a while, you'll learn its peculiar and sometimes hidden fundamental elements that make it both viable and potent. You might not be able to name them or be sure which is more important than another, but you cannot mistake them for anything but fundamental. Take the popular board game Monopoly, the most successful modern-day board game. The board has four sides of ten spaces, just the right size for a game played with two die; you pass "Go" seemingly just when you need another $200 dollars, but not before you have to walk the gauntlet of Boardwalk and Park Place; and those under-appreciated railroads turn out to be nice cash cows.

THE BUSINESS FAD GAME

Likewise the Business Fad Game has its own fundamentals, and they are three: Possibility of Success, Security of Fashion, and the Law of Averages. The Possibility of Success lures management to sign up for the latest guru's program because these cures, when successful, supposedly make the company a lot of money. It is easy to convince yourself that a potential 80% failure rate is tolerable if the upside is sufficiently attractive.

Of course, the downside has to be protected. Given that most of these programs will surely fail, the game relies on its second fundamental to minimize the impact of a loss: Security of Fashion. If "everyone" is signing up, then it's easy to rationalize that there must be something to this new program. Besides, even if you don't know much about it, it's very fashionable these days. If you fail, you'll feel safe because you'll be in the company of many of your industry peers wearing the same fashion.

The second fundamental shows up in polite business conversations that go something like this:

"So, how's your LMNOP Program going? . . . What, you aren't doing LMNOP? Everyone is doing LMNOP. I read just last week that Amalgamated Armotronics improved their quality 200% in six months and won the LMNOP Award. Their new president got a huge bonus. Didn't you see him featured in this month's issue of *Dysfunctional Trends*?"

Any red-blooded manager wouldn't be caught dead without an LMNOP Program. No matter how hideous the latest fashion looks on him, he wants it. After all, everyone's wearing it.

The third fundamental—the Law of Averages—ensures that the downside consequences of the game go unnoticed or can be explained away, on average, the same way a statistical average hides individual performance. A product of fashion has to be relatively harmless in order to be sustainable. Sure, some men with robust waists shouldn't wear the latest European-style bathing suit, and some women past their prime should perhaps forego the latest skirt style. While certain individuals may look foolish, the harm these fashions cause is limited, superficial, and lost when we calculate the overall impact on humanity.

Likewise, the business fad game is sustainable because we think that if harm comes from it, it's minimal—sort of like being caught wearing casual wear to a cocktail party. The Law of Averages says a game like this must *appear* harmless on average. On average most managements feel obligated to try something to improve performance and profitability. On average if the staff wasn't involved in one improvement program, it would be involved in some other improvement program. While these fads may lower efficiency in the overall economy, they are a part of the way we do business. On average you don't miss wealth you never knew you had. However, on an individual company basis—the place where each one of us lives—following a fad can be devastating. Unlike an entertaining child's game, the business fad game has serious individual consequences. That's where the symbolism between parlor games and business fads breaks down. No one loses his job if he loses a Monopoly game.

BREAKING OUT

Unless you find a way to break the business fad's life cycle, your future will be dotted with endless attempts at installing the latest program that bubbles up from the business fad industry. Laying aside the question which particular program might be right for you, we first need to know if there is something that can separate the few successes from the many failures. As we discuss later in detail, *no* fundamental change will occur if the threat to your company is vague and lifeless, if insiders believe that your company is inherently better than its competitors, or if you remain convinced that you and the people around you are doing the best job possible.

We aren't saying it will be hard to change if you lack a clear, overwhelming threat. We're saying it will be impossible. You will have to face near catastrophe and a clear, identifiable enemy before significant change occurs. Then after you survive the war, you'll need enough strength left to re-build before the next onslaught. For example, take IBM's well-publicized troubles of the early 1990s. Many outside the company recognized the signs of crisis years before, as did a few insiders. The board eventually had to bring in an outsider. Only someone like Louis Gerstner could paint a stark picture of reality for the majority of insiders who had dozed off listening to stories of ancient success. Although his work at the time of this writing was far from finished, he admitted that he was lucky to have a real crisis to get people's attention and that IBM still had core strengths upon which to re-build.

The IBM story contrasts with the tale of Westinghouse. Concurrent and coincidentally with IBM's troubles, Westinghouse faced convincing evidence that something was very wrong with its basic business. Outsider Mike Jordan was brought in, but substantial changes were still a long way off after two years of effort. Jordan's plan had two fatal flaws: (1) insufficient attention to communicating the unequivocal need for change and (2) Jordan's reported conviction that the Westinghouse "culture" was the culprit and could be changed by seeding the headquarter's staff with marketing- and financial-types. Their inability to communicate the depth and breadth of the crisis meant that the entrenched troops remained unconvinced that they had to change their way of doing business. The second flaw meant that Jordan defined Westinghouse's "culture" as the change objective. This objective implies that Westinghouse management was going to turn the company around by emphasizing a presumed weakness—the lack of entrepreneurial, market-driven focus—while ignoring a core strength—its technical bureaucracy. Not coincidentally, a corporate culture make-over was one of the change programs fashionable during the Westinghouse turn-around attempt. Westinghouse will become another story of business fads gone mad, unless, of course, it has a serendipitous run of good luck. In that case corporate culture change programs will become all the rage.

Although always real, not every threat is as in-your-face as IBM's or Westinghouse's. The difference between success and failure of many improvement initiatives is not the change initiative itself, but the creative leader implementing it. This person sees the threat more clearly than others, energetically describes the faceless enemy to others, and engages battle before his peers would. Whether you find one of the popular, off-the-shelf business fads attractive or see all of them as last Sunday's left-overs, you yourself will have to make your change program work by using your intelligence, by applying the force of your personality, and by persisting via hard, almost never-ending work. This book is about the nature of that work and its rewards.

---

[1]*Throughout this book we will state many facts without retribution. We find that such pedantic attention is both boring and meaningless. Many established facts (e.g., Elvis is dead) are disputed vigorously and endlessly. Many falsehoods (e.g., technological change rates are at their highest in recorded history) become popularly accepted facts and never challenged. Anyone can dispute that self-reported failure rates vary between 60 to 80 percent by attacking methodology, but that only obscures the point. Whatever the* real *failure rate, it's high, and for those who fail, it's immaterial.*

2

Chapter 2

The Maze

Look back at the first paragraph of this book. Seems topical, doesn't it? It isn't. The opening paragraph could have been written 10 years ago as well as 10 years in the future. Why can't we escape this maze?

WHAT'S IN A NAME?

For some clues, let's look at how our era is popularly characterized. You are constantly told that this is "The Computer Age" or "The Information Revolution". What's in a name? More than you think. Names have implied, unspoken meanings. Remember learning in the seventh grade about "The Age of the Steam Engine" and its variant "The Industrial Revolution". The first variant (Steam Engine) characterized the machine whose principal impact on society was embodied in the second variant (Industrial Revolution). It's a visual mnemonic. See the steam engine, see industry.

Like the term "Age of the Steam Engine", the term "Computer Age" refers to the predominate *machine* of our time. But the symmetry doesn't hold with the second variant. Unlike the word *industrial* as used in the "Industrial Revolution", the word *information* refers not to the machine's impact on society but to the substance *in* the machine. It's like calling the Age of the Steam Engine the "Steam Revolution," but for obvious reasons we don't. It's redundant. Then why call our era the "Information

Revolution"? We shouldn't. It is an impotent descriptor implying content and impact are the same thing, which of course they're not.

THE FAD FACTORY

So what is the impact of the computer's content on our society? While it has obviously lowered costs in many industries, in the world of business management it has lead to the ubiquitous management fad. Fads are unsustainable unless they can quickly generate a critical mass of followers. To reach out to this critical mass business fads need a really fast and ubiquitous communications system, which itself depends on cheap computer technology. Furthermore, business fads need computers to sustain nationwide, targeted marketing efforts and to maintain efficient "information" cloning—the core manufacturing activity of the business fad industry.

What is important to understanding the age of the steam engine is neither a grasp of the machine nor thermodynamics, but an appreciation of how the machine was used. What's important to understanding our age is not a comprehension of the computing machine nor the information in it, but an awareness of how its output is used. Future generations of managers will not marvel at the computer any more than you marvel at the steam engine. Most likely when they look back at us, they'll even forget to put the computer in the picture, just as you forget to put the steam engine in your mind's eye when you think about the great textile, steel, oil, shipbuilding and railroad industries of the past. Instead, you see the skies darkened with the soot of work and bodies hardened by a life of toil. They will not blame the computer for the excesses of the past anymore than we blame the steam engine for the terrible working conditions of the late 19th century. History assigns credit and blame squarely on the shoulders of *people* who applied innovation, not the innovation itself.

Your life and times are defined by the actual, real work you do, not by the machines you do it with nor the content of the material you work. It's the real value you leave behind that counts. Following a fad for fashion's sake leaves a sterile legacy.

IN THE MAZE

When did the Era of the Business Fad begin, and how do you know you're in it? We need to go back to a previous era to understand how we got where we are today. You've read or heard about the golden age of the post-World War II business boom. Instead of re-living the myths of that era, let's review a few facts. New businesses were forming at an incredible rate because established businesses could not create enough jobs for all the returning GIs. Because their war-time experiences taught them how to overcome almost any obstacle, many of them did what they had to do to make a living: They started their own businesses. They augmented their Army/Navy leadership skills with on-the-job trial-and-error. Many failed, but those who survived were quick, smart learners. They did not learn their business lessons from following *Wall Street Journal* articles about the trials and tribulations of Ford, Mobil, or General Electric. That world was irrelevant. Survival was the name of the game. At that time business tended to be regional. If you had a business problem, you sought help from those around you. Local business leaders, your family, your customers, your suppliers, and (surprise!) your competitors were your best sources of information. A good idea was a good idea no matter where it came from.

Many of those post-World War II business leaders began to retire in the 1980s. Typically, they sold their companies to others who had a "strategic acquisition plan". The new owners brought in bright, professional managers who in many cases were trained or influenced by business schools.

People like yourself. But American business schools by and large teach business by carving it up into disciplines like finance, marketing and accounting. When they teach general management skills, they rely on the "case method." This teaching technique leads to a management-by-case mind-set. When these ideas escape campus, they become management fads, infecting a lot of otherwise normal and even gifted people.

But let's not get carried away. Business schools are not the problem of poor corporate performance any more than American engineering schools are the cause of poorly designed highways. However, these schools have a tendency to reinforce a certain way of thinking. This type of thinking, when turned loose on the world, looks for ways to validate itself.

Joining business schools on the list of business fad enablers is an *eminence grice* that gives the fad industry a nearly everlasting life: the general business press. Journalists face a relentless, all-absorbing, grinding problem of how to fill the white space or dead air between advertisements. Thoughtful consideration of tactical business problems is hard to communicate. Simple, monotonous patterns proffering the latest fad answers are easier to write, easier to edit, easier to repeat and easier to swallow. The journalists' challenge is to sell papers, magazines, books, and television programs in an increasingly saturated, distracted market. Business journalists build a world of fiction similar to made-for-television, "reality-based" programming. They should be required to put a disclaimer with each piece like Hollywood does on many of its products: "Any resemblance between the characters and scenes depicted in this work and any real life situation is purely coincidental. This story is a total fabrication."

When pundits tag our life and times with words like the "Computer Age" or the "Information Revolution," they are guilty of infecting us with provincial, in-bred ideas and meaningless meanings. If you are trying to escape the maze in which you find yourself, you'll get no boost from framing your situation using these feeble terms. Instead, frame it in terms of the tyranny of the business fad. That way you'll get a foothold on the way out.

ESCAPING THE MAZE

The business press is not the only vehicle used by the American business fad industry, it's just the most obvious and persistent one. Finding your way out of the maze of business fads and fakes takes more than seeing through such self-promotion. After all, this maze mutates into a new form every two years or so, adding a new corridor, mirror or passage leading back to itself. Finding your way out takes fundamental problem-solving skills. You have to be able to look at the once-familiar suspiciously or at least in a different light. You have to be able to distinguish from two or more seemingly identical choices. You have to be able to back out of dead-ends without running into yourself going in. A map can be helpful, and you might suspect that this book is one. It is not. Maps are easy to come by; map-reading skills are in short supply. Even skilled maze-makers themselves become trapped in their own mazes, unable to get out even though they think they know everything about their creation.

What you need more than a map is cross-country trekking skills. You need to be able to find old, faithful but seldom-used paths. You need to know which places to avoid even though they are not marked as dangerous. You need to spot false turns, dead-ends, and drop-offs before you reach them. An accomplished trekker knows that few maps show this kind of detail. A map is only a start; a successful journey depends on decisions made after leaving civilization behind. This book will help you become that experienced, knowledgeable and mature trekker.

Back in this world general managers, presidents, CEOs and other management generalists like yourself avoid the traps of the maze by relying on six fundamental skills. These fundamentals do not include quality program skills, although the quality of your product and service can hardly be ignored. They don't even include team-building skills, although building teams is a necessary activity. Reengineering or right-sizing is not on the list, although improved operational efficiency is the tangible result of applying fundamental general management skills. Instead, the fundamental skills allow you to see through the maze to extract the real, underlying business ideas in each of these topical management salves. It's time for us to reject the fad mongers in favor of more critical skills. The legacy of your generation of business leaders depends on it.

3

Chapter 3

The Fundamentals

When you meet new people, they invariably ask you what you do for a living. If you say you are a surgeon, they immediately form a picture in their minds. They see you using your skills cutting people open, re-arranging what you find, sewing them up, and seeing them through recovery. You and your new friends use euphemisms to describe what you do, but regardless of the words most people will form a fairly straightforward and graphic picture of you at work. If you say you're a pilot, they see you using your skills to guide a plane full of people or cargo through a complex air-traffic control system so that you get from Point A to Point B. They see the plane, airport, and uniform. What if you say you're a "manager"? What picture do your new friends paint? What skills do they think you have? What does your finished work look like to them? You try to explain yourself: "I'm good with people. I understand numbers. I solve problems." You get a polite but nonplussed "Oh, I see."

To make your life easier, instead of saying you're a manager, you might tell them what you used to be, as if you still did that job. You'll say you're an engineer, an accountant, a salesman, a lawyer, or a programmer. You know if you chose a familiar title, they'll be able to form a fairly coherent mental picture of your work without much explanation, even if the picture is wrong. For example, if you own your own company, you feel safe to say that you own a company. People understand ownership: They see someone in an office reading mail, taking phone calls, taking early lunches, and taking off in the afternoon. The conversation then turns to what the *company* does, not what *you* the owner do. The introduction gets over the first hurdle nicely. If you can't claim to be the president or owner, but nonetheless have similar general management responsibilities, more likely than not you'll mention your former profession.

There is nothing wrong with your little white lie, reclaiming your previous profession just so you can keep party conversation going. However, some managers explain their work in terms of their technical expertise because they've never come to terms with being a general manager. At the end of most days they feel they have accomplished something. But ask them to explain *how* they do what they do and what *exactly* it is they do, they'll only be able to relate to the technical side of their job, which is about 20 percent of it. That 20 percent claims 100 percent of their attention because the technical side is the only part of their work they know. When faced with a critical management task outside of their technical realm, they find themselves lacking the other necessary skills. They come to lean on ready-made, fashionable business fads, joining the ranks of camp followers rather than leaders. It doesn't have to be that way.

WHAT'S UP, DOC?

Before we can list the fundamental skills of managers, we have to define their job. That's fairly simple: Managers run the business. How do they do that? They ensure that the operating systems defining their department or business are designed, installed, and maintained. After all, what is a business if not a collection of agreements between people concerning how to organize their individual work such that they can sell a product or service for a profit? These agreements are collected into various *systems*—the order entry system, the financial reporting system, the production control system. ***System*** comes from the ancient Greek *syn* + *histanai*, meaning "to cause to stand." Likewise, translated into the business world, the system is "that upon which the business stands". Without a systematic way of doing work, a business cannot stand. Someone has to be responsible for making sure the system works, and that someone is management. Managers are no strangers to systems and regularly refer to them every day. They are not mysterious conventions invented by the people long forgotten. They are alive.

It's popular to think that the system belongs to everyone, not to management. However, individuals who work *in* a system are at a disadvantage when it comes to working *on* the system. Working on the system requires straddling the line between work as it is done today and work as you want it done in the future. This maneuver takes a suite of complex skills that are accumulated over time, that are reinforced by constant application, and that are supported by appropriate rewards. If you take someone who has been working in the system and give them the responsibility and authority to work on the system, but deny them adequate time to learn their new job, deny them the opportunity to try different approaches to changing the system, and deny them a new role in the new system by indicating that they will return to their "old" job when the project is finished, you are finished.

The job of general management is neither a part-time assignment nor a temporary occupation. The system upon which your business is built needs constant care and professional attention. To understand these needs and to be able to provide for them takes the thoughtful training and insight provided by pursuing these six fundamental skills:

- Profit fixation
- Technical literacy
- Change dynamics insight
- Policy and procedure comprehension
- Decision theory knowledge
- Character duality

WHAT'S FUNDAMENTAL ABOUT FUNDAMENTALS?

We will flesh out these fundamental skills in a minute, but first we want to explore what it means when something is a fundamental skill. A ***skill*** is a "developed aptitude or ability to do something competently." If fundamental, such a skill determines "essential structure or function". So by definition these six fundamental skills define the essence of what it means to be a good manager.

Moreover, any skill takes practice to develop and requires repetition to maintain. For instance, a pilot must fly to keep sharp. A surgeon must perform surgery to remain proficient. Not many of us would board a plane knowing the pilot hadn't flown for six months. Few of us would be happy having a surgeon cut us open if he hadn't performed surgery for a year. All professions demand a significant level of attention to some set of fundamental skills. Why are employees empowered to work on the system if they lack a complete set of fundamental skills? Why are newly-minted general managers expected to bring an undefined skill set to a poorly-defined job? And why do managers expect themselves to remain competent if they neglect their fundamental skills?

IS THIS JUST ANOTHER LIST?

Look at the skills inventory again: profit, technical literacy, change dynamics, policy and procedure, decision theory, and duality. Although it looks like a list, it is a collection. Like any collection it has to be seen as a whole, not as a pile of individual pieces. A common demand of art collectors, for instance, is that their collection be kept together when they bequeath it to a museum. The same applies to this collection of fundamentals. You can't divide it. No one item can be taken from it without changing the appearance and meaning of the remaining items. One of the reasons fads fail is that they take one of these fundamentals, adorn it with all sorts of jargon and superfluous activities, and claim that if you apply it in a program of good hygiene and regular professional care your problems will be solved. They rarely are.

We are not claiming any new insights with this list. Fashionable management fads invariably claim that they have discovered a new truth. After you slog through their program, the truth you find is neither novel nor profound. At its core is one, and only one, of these six ideas. While the fundamentals we present in this book are not new (if they were they wouldn't be fundamental), our collection is displayed and explained in a coherent framework.

Even though we haven't yet explained what is behind our six fundamentals, you should be suspicious of anything that claims to be fundamental, much less something that claims to be fundamental to a discipline that many people think is hardly a profession at all, or if it is, it is one that can be learned on-the-job. After all, what can be so hard about a job whose title uses the word "general"? The fact is being a good manager is a difficult job, and it requires fundamental skills. But how will you *know* after reading our descriptions of these fundamentals that they are indeed fundamental?

The practical, real-world test of any fundamental idea is finding out what happens if we ignore it. For example, take the ancient philosophical argument about whether reality is real or just a construct. As a child many of us thought about this, too. How could we tell if reality was real or if the world as we perceived it had no substance? In other words, we wondered whether the world was put here for our individual entertainment or if it was something bigger. That's a no-brainer for philosophers calling themselves realists. It's pretty much a no-brainer for the rest of us, too. The simple test is that if you ignore any of the fundamental elements of reality, they will hurt you. Suppose you want to test the substance of reality by stepping off a cliff. If you take one step over the edge, the practical result for the rest of us is that you're dead. For those of us who remain behind, reality is a fundamental truth. It is the same for any list of fundamentals, whether it is the one we present here or it's someone else's. You face metaphorical death if you ignore them.

The current enchantment with self-directed, empowered teams is a good test of fundamentalism. This fad's premise is that the best method for solving problems is gathering together those people with intimate understanding of the situation, training them in problem-solving techniques, and letting them loose with little direction. They're allowed to define their own problems and generate their own solutions. Tales of success and triumph of this problem-solving method saturate the business press. Whole companies have been saved and industries revitalized! But: Is knowing how to assemble self-directed teams a fundamental skill? As you read on, it will become obvious that while teams-building might be a skill preferred by some, it is not a fundamental skill required by all. It doesn't represent an essential structure or function of general management; it represents a style. If you remove this skill from the face of the earth, you won't perish. But if you ignore any of the tried and true *fundamentals* we present, you're in real trouble.

What follows is a simple sketch of each of the six fundamentals. We'll give you enough to wet your lips, but not enough to get you to the first landmark shown on your map. This is your shake-down cruise, so don't worry if these initial explanations seem incomplete. They're not intended to last an entire trip. The chapters that follow will provide the sustenance you need to be comfortable during your trek out of the maze.

PROFIT

The primary focus of general management is profit.

This is so fundamental to business it seems trite and out of place in a list of fundamental general management skills. Of all the fundamentals we discussed while writing this book, the decision to include profit generated more disputes because it's so fundamental that it should be axiomatic. But think about your own experience. When was the last time someone mentioned profit when discussing competing solutions to a problem? Sure, you heard a lot of words about increasing market share, improving efficiency, reducing redundancy, and enhancing quality, but when was the last time you actually heard the word "profit"? You probably can't remember, and if you do, either it was a rare event or you work in a rare environment.

This absence of the word profit is not a trivial matter. It is not merely an oversight. It is as if a mariner lost his map and compass. He might get to landfall by way of the sun and stars, but it would be blind luck if he arrived at his chosen destination. In our case, if such a fundamental concept as profit is not spoken aloud, often and vigorously, its power is soon lost. As we said, because the profit motive is the bedrock of business, it almost didn't make our list of fundamentals. But its absence from contemporary business vocabulary demands that it be on the list and have a special place: the cardinal skill. That we had to include a skill akin to breathing is a sad testimony to the extent that management-by-fad has replaced management-by-fundamental.

TECHNICAL LITERACY

It's fashionable these days to insist that general managers don't need to know the technical foundations of the company, division or department they lead. This notion is one of the biggest intellectual frauds of the past 20 years. That people readily accepted this rationalization for technical incompetence in the general management function shows that, like any fad, this specious idea had a ready market.

As we explain later, your level of technical competency need not reach that of your most proficient technician, engineer or scientist. In fact, it defeats the idea of division of labor if you expect yourself to stay abreast of any but the major technical developments impacting your business. However, general management does require something called "technical literacy," a kind of knowledge readily available to anyone with the basic intelligence required of successful managers.

CHANGE DYNAMICS

Controlling the direction, pace, and impact of change is such a fundamental management skill that it, too, is in danger of becoming a fad pushed by experts with ready-made programs. Remember, the core concept of a business fad isn't necessarily bad. It's that the fad overwhelms the fundamental ingredient to such an extent that the original concept is unrecognizable.

Change dynamics include issues of "culture" (another overused, misused, misconstrued, and generally abused concept), human and organizational behavior, and change measurement. Without a coherent framework explaining how people and organizations change, you won't be able to manage the process consistently and effectively. While researchers can spend their lives plowing this fertile field, you'll be interested in learning just a few basics of how companies change.

POLICY AND PROCEDURE

It's disappointing that many otherwise competent managers believe that establishing policy and procedures is a necessary evil. The arguments against writing policy and documenting practice are easily recounted. You probably have your own list you've collected over the years. They include: "We do things differently every time." "We're a unique company in a unique industry. Policies and procedures don't work for us." "We don't have time to write everything down." "We don't want to become burdened by paper." "If you start down that road, you'll need a piece of paper to turn off the lights."

People who shudder at the thought of reducing policy and procedure to paper, nevertheless, expect their paychecks to be issued on time, error-free. They expect to get consistent service from the grocery store. They demand their government services be cheaper and more efficient. You can eventually get them to admit that if they didn't get their checks on time, their groceries bagged properly, or their mail delivered every day, the solution would include establishing a few procedures and keeping some records. Beneath our denial, we know that without paper and pencil (or their replacement the computer) a business couldn't run.

So, let's agree: The debate is not about whether records, procedures, and policy are necessary but about how much is necessary. Taking the position that reducing policy and procedures to paper is *de facto* a bad idea is a non-starter. To overcome this fashionable, knee-jerk attitude, you'll need to learn how to determine what must be documented and what doesn't. As you put these ideas to work, you'll begin to appreciate that written policy and procedure can make you money.

DECISION THEORY

At first blush it's strange to think that you have to learn to think. But of the many skills we must learn in life, our teachers do the poorest job teaching us to think. Organizational behaviorists and clinical psychologists have a name for the process of thinking about alternatives and choosing one over the other: Decision Theory. Many of their ideas about how good people make bad decisions are perhaps the most useful tools you'll ever learn as a general manager. You'll learn some of the more prevalent decision theory traps. You'll be astounded that by merely changing the way you ask questions you'll get better information and have higher confidence in your decisions.

DUALITY

Duality is "the state of being of two irreducible modes." For general managers this duality comes from having to respond to the needs of the group as well as the needs of individual people, including themselves. All good general managers we've known have had very personal relationships at every level within the organization. Paradoxically, these same general managers still respected that relic of neanderthal management, the chain of command. Walking this tightrope takes perception and control of the dual role of leader and comrade. Recognizing and mastering duality is a learned skill.

For a manager, learning these fundamental skills is equivalent to a survivalist learning cross-country trekking skills. Maps are helpful and sometimes crucial, but not absolutely essential. What is essential is a good grounding in fundamental skills. They alone ensure that you will avoid running in circles, exhausting yourself, lost in a maze.

4

Chapter 4

The "P" Word

Among a collection of fundamental skills there's always one cardinal skill. For instance, all baseball players except pitchers have to have a "quick bat". Regardless of position, if they are going to hit in the big leagues, they have to learn to get their bats around very, very quickly. A big league pitch comes at them so fast that the time between their decision to swing and the swing itself is nearly instantaneous. Sure, ball players need other skills too, but without this cardinal skill, they won't hold their job. So what is the fundamental skill of really, really good general managers that without it they wouldn't be able to hold their jobs? Their ability to keep focused on profit.

VJ DAY

The goal of your professional life's work is generating profit, period. That seems like a straight-forward ideal, yet for some, profit is less than virtuous. Sure, not all people pursue profit as their life's work. There are plenty of other noble goals to work toward. But the cold, hard fact is that in this society most of us work for "the spread". Once you are profitable, and consistently so, you can do all of the things wealth allows, including rejecting it. Most of us would like to be wealthy enough to reject wealth. But until then, all of us are one month away from the virtual jungle.

People are always trying to find ways to avoid saying the P-word. This is similar to many American politicians' reluctance to embrace some other indelicate words. During Clinton's presidency a small flap developed during the planning for anniversary celebrations of the victory of Allied forces over Japan during World War II. Mr. Clinton was purported to be reluctant to refer to that historic day as "VJ Day", believing to do so would be discourteous towards the Japanese. During a briefing a White House aid was quoted as saying defensively, "VJ Day, VJ Day, VJ Day, VJ Day, VJ Day! There, I said it five times in a row."

Is the word "profit" your "VJ Day"? Do you have trouble saying the word in polite conversation? Many aren't comfortable using it. Given a choice they'd rather defend the righteousness of a male-dominated society than defend the virtues of a profit-driven motive. Unfortunately, this politically-correct discrimination has a deadly side-affect. You're avoiding using the P-word where and when you absolutely must—the impolite office arena. Not only should you use "profit," you should use it until the scab of political correctness falls off.

Recently we met with a group of owners and managers of an emerging technology company. We were discussing the role of policy and procedures. When we asked them to list the reasons they were spending their time at this meeting, only one of the nine mentioned profit, and then only obliquely. The sad thing is this response is typical. Few business people keep a portrait of profit anywhere in their foreground. What they do is use lots of surrogates for profit. They'll say their "new" initiative will improve customer service, reduce overhead, increase sales, improve quality, facilitate teamwork, or reduce cycle time. Never does it occur to them to say the new program will increase profit.

Why is it so important for managers to be more comfortable with the P-word? Because a surrogate is never as good as the original—never. Why? Because when the surrogate goal replaces the real goal, you have a subsequent loss in focus. Eventually a fad tag like TQM, ISO, or reengineering replaces the goal. Severed from the real goal of making a profit, these management fads take on a life of their own and profit suffers.

PROFIT IS NOT A FOUR-LETTER WORD

All business failures are ultimately about losing focus on profit; all business successes are ultimately about sustaining a focus on profit. All other explanations are merely expansions of this theme. So if you find that surrogate concepts have taken the place of profit in your business vocabulary, you have a serious infection. You have to get over it, but how?

Use "profit" in *every* answer to *every* business question for a solid week or two or three. You'll be surprised how easy it is to start every answer with "Let's discuss how each alternative affects profits." Eventually, this little exercise will become second nature, and you'll learn to demand that people frame their alternatives in terms of improving profit right from the start. While it will certainly feel good to become focused on why everyone comes to work in the morning, this transformation will help your technicians communicate in a common but richer language. Unknowingly, they'll quit treating "profit" as a four-letter word. Eventually, they'll have no problem using it in polite conversation.

Let's look at an actual example of how focusing on profit can clarify a problem. A client's computer system operator claimed that the current stand-alone computers in the design department needed to be replaced with a network. She said that the new system would improve efficiency because design engineers would no longer have to trade floppies, and, therefore, she would eliminate the confusion and cost surrounding the question of which drawing was the latest. All that was fine and good, but several other questions begged to be answered. Later we'll discuss the importance of demanding alternatives; for now we want to show how important it is to ask questions about profit. Before asking whether better procedures could solve these problems and increase efficiency, we asked, "How much money will you make from the investment? How many months will it take to pay it back? What's the primary source of the profit from this cost?" If your staff is like this one, they are used to presenting their ideas in terms other than profit. They'll be at a loss to answer these questions at first. If after struggling with the answer they cannot develop a rational set of numbers showing how the investment in new technology will make money, then you shouldn't approve it.

In our example, the system operator's first stab was to quantify the un-quantifiable. She made some assumptions about how often files were misplaced, how often the wrong file was updated, and how long it took to swap diskettes between users. Most of the evidence was anecdotal, but at least it was a start. We then asked her to set up a rational method for gathering actual data about these activities. By then she was well on her way to developing a robust, profit-centered picture of "improving efficiency."

In the end the investment in the network was solely justified on standardizing print size and reducing paper costs. Nuts and bolts, dollars and cents. The fact that other problems might be solved did not enter into the equation. Efficiency improvements and better communications are hard to quantify and easy to dispute. The real value of this particular investment was not in the network but in new printing technology that required a network environment to work and therefore generate a profit.

This is a good place to introduce a theme that we'll come back to later from another direction. It is our experience that when investments in new technologies, especially computer technologies, do not return money to the bottom line they do so for the same principal reason. No one took the time to apply the same discipline to these decisions as they would to buying a new machine for the production line. The power of the first fundamental derives from being applied consistently, over a long period of time, to all decisions. Decisions—about hiring, about firing, about expanding a product line, about dropping a line, about setting up a booth at a convention, about increasing employee benefits, about decreasing benefits, about outsourcing, about starting a new management program, about hiring your brother-in-law, about resurfacing the parking lot, about holding a Christmas party—all need to be framed in terms of increasing your profits. Can't justify it? Then don't do it.

Think about how you can justify the value of a company picnic, using dollars and cents. In other words, how does a picnic paid by the company make money for the shareholders? Your answer better be "Yes" and with an exact amount. This, of course, is a radical (some would say bogus) exercise. But if focusing on profit is a cardinal skill, we can't shy away from those sticky problems that reside at the margins of business and life. Besides, you have to show yourself that fixating on profit is really a fundamental skill and that you can do it. But remember what we said about the list. It's a collection, and no one element stands alone. That does not mean that one element can be ignored since others will fill the gap, nor that one is so powerful in certain circumstances that it holds sway over the others. A collection of fundamentals cannot be affected by "special situations." It means that when you work a problem you have to apply all the skills in order to solve it creatively, completely, and absolutely. If, after thinking about quantifying the profit of a company picnic, you come up empty-handed, don't worry. The other fundamentals will help you out.

5

Chapter 5

Your Second Language

The second fundamental skill of general management is technical literacy. General managers must be able to cut to the chase on technical issues quickly, and this means that they have to retain a minimum technical grasp in a wide range of applied disciplines. Why is this skill, among the many that good general managers must possess, a fundamental one? Because a general manager is his company's techno-linguist. To be able to get things done as a general manager you have to communicate your ideas to technicians using language you both understand. But it's your job, not theirs, to be multilingual because you're the one who has to mediate between competing sets of technicians who speak different technical languages.

This faculty is different from the technicians'. For example, to live and work in a foreign country you have to speak the language. You don't—and won't—speak as well as a native, nor are you expected to. So relax if you're technically ignorant in some facets of the work around you. There are ways to pick it up, and we'll introduce you to them. But before we go on to outline how this can be done, we need to show why techno-literacy is a fundamental skill.

This idea—that general managers' jobs depend on their ability to translate technical expectations across functional boundaries—flies in the face of a twenty-year movement to remove the technical component from general management. The idea that general managers needn't know the business, understand the core technology, nor have a feel for the market has been a popular one. It's said that after all, managers just pull the strings. So the only fundamental skill managers need are people skills so that they can manipulate people. Yea, right. A music conductor doesn't need to know how to play an instrument, doesn't need to understand acoustics, and need not know how to please the audience.

This mindless drivel has been taken to the mountain top, clothed in latest business fashion by a recent and insanely popular book claiming to illustrate the common traits of really, really successful people. A whole consulting practice has been built around the implication that by copying these traits, you, too, can become fantastically successful. Some *Fortune 500* companies are inculcating their people with this new business religion.

Interestingly, when this New Wave book first came out it was aimed *primarily* at the self-help market and could be found in the personal improvement section of bookstores, next to such self-help classics as "I'm Okay, You're Screwed Up" and "If Life Gives You a Lemon, Demand a Refund." But there's a basic problem with trying to copy character traits. You can't. By definition *character* is something you have, not something you build through exercise. Everyone has an opinion about character formation, but no one knows for sure how we develop our own distinctive character. Some speculate the process is pretty much complete by the age of five or six; others assign its completion later in life. But most agree that character is certainly set by the time we start to work for a living. So you can no more become a successful person by trying to copy a set of character traits than you can become a professional athlete by copying an exercise regimen.

It's a myth that management style determines management success. The fact is that really, really successful business people are the most diverse group on the planet.

The fact is that the typical successful person does not exist. Taskmaster or integrator, you'll find plenty of people who like your style and want to help you reach your goal, but only if you know who you are, what you want, and how to communicate it. However, regardless of your style or character, in this world if you're technically illiterate, you won't be able to talk to many of the people that determine your success. If you can't talk to them, you can't get any real work done.

ROUND UP THE USUAL EXCUSES

Most of us come to general management via success in another function, such as sales, finance, engineering, operations, administration, or law. Up to that point we've spent a considerable amount of our lives building technical expertise, which in our new job as general manager will only contribute at most 20 percent to our continuing success. Unfortunately, even though those skills have little to do with success in our new job, we find ourselves falling back on our old profession. After all that's where we feel comfortable. Most general managers with engineering backgrounds have their best relationship with the engineering department. It's the same for the ex-salesperson, ex-lawyer, and ex-chief financial officer.

Managers try to ignore functions they know little about. Fear is a natural result of ignorance, and overcoming ignorance is hard, painful work. They believe that since they're the manager they're paid to have thousand-dollar answers. They figure if they don't have quick, glib answers, then they're frauds. This makes some general managers avoid functional experts since these experts sound like they just got off a plane from Katmandu.

As general managers it's easy to be convinced that the more arcane functions can be left to the "experts". We'll just rely on our good judgment about people to keep us out of trouble. Besides, there are a lot of apologists who rationalize our behavior. Everyone says technology is so complicated these days that no one person can possibly understand it all. Anyway, isn't empowerment about letting people work out their own problems? It's really not our job anyway to babysit these people we've hired. They're adults. We pay them good money for them to know their jobs. But wait . . . look at the reality of business and people. Empowerment as applied in the real world is mostly superficial. For the most part the only functions that are empowered to work on their own problems are those about which the general manager knows little. The functions in which he is versatile are kept on a short leash. If the general manager took empowerment to its logical conclusion, he would reduce his job to inane boosterism. Boy, now that's a job I want!

The hot, harsh heat of reality makes these excuses and inconsistencies wither away. While it is true that technology can be at times unfathomable, its *effect* on your organization is real and easily comprehended. The corporate battlefield is littered with companies that blew apart at the seams because their managers were functioning techno-illiterates. Looking back at the destruction, the managers' abandonment of the battlefield for the rear bunker was obvious to the people who were left leaderless. Many companies tread water while trying out different general managers, all who look like they have the "right" character but don't have a clue about running the business.

Right about now, you're saying, "Okay, so I need to know a lot of stuff about a lot of stuff. And I feel like I should have known it by now. But I don't. So where does that leave me?" Where most of your peers are, but in a better position than you were yesterday. By this time you've unearthed several facts. You know that much of what passes for conventional business wisdom leads to fashionable failure. You know that profits are what should get your attention, and you know that most people who work for you are looking for guidance from you and will do your bidding if you stay true to yourself. Those who won't help you will have to be identified and unloaded, but more on that skill later.

What you don't realize is that you already have most of the skills you need to be a good manager. They've just been overwhelmed by the myth machine of American business experts.

IMPROVING YOUR TECHNO-LITERACY

So what's your exercise program to improve your techno-literacy? First, honesty with your people and yourself, followed by developing an action plan to fix the problem. Write down your blind spots when it comes to key technologies in your company. For example, suppose you don't know how to run a lathe, but you've got 16 of them working 20 hours a day? Honesty really is the best policy in this case because everyone knows you don't know your ear from a hole in the ground when it comes to these machines, so why not admit it out loud and get on with learning the language? By admitting the obvious, you replace fear and resentment with knowledge and respect of those around you. There will always be someone who will gloat, but, by and large, you'll be removing an issue standing between you and success.

You'll find your people are eager to show you what they know, and if they're not, find some who are. Got a union to work around? Now you're making excuses. The shop steward knows you're not training to take someone's job away. If you can't get him to help you, your union problems are going to kill you anyway. One approach might be to ask a lead machinist to put together a simple program to bring you up to speed on routine tasks, or you could take a correspondence course or two on machine tool design.

You say you don't have time for this? We've got news for you. The practical, technical learning of general management never ends. It's a part of your job. It's part of the job no one told you about. It's the part that if you had a job description would fall under the topic "Training." If you don't have time for learning more about your base technology, you don't have time for your job. So figure out what the lowest value activity is that you do today, stop doing it, and replace it with real value activities. What about going out to the shop or the lab during your lunch instead of reading the *Wall Street Journal* or *Barron's*? After all, all you're getting from them is fashion ideas.

6

Chapter 6

Times They Are a Changin'

Alexander the Great conquered much of the known western world in ten years. Nearly one-quarter of the population of Europe died during the first Black Plague that lasted four years. The great wealth machine of the Yankee seafaring towns lasted a generation, the Pony Express less than two years. World War II lasted about five years after the U.S. declared war on Japan. Each generation living during these times was convinced that the "rate of change" was the greatest the world had seen. However, today's popular business press claims that today's business leader has to manage change like no other generation before him. A quick review of U.S. business history, or any history, shows that the presumption of "an era of change like no other" is a false but comforting myth. Believing that your generation alone is facing a unique challenge is a hearty bowl of comfort when you're on a diet of misfortune. It's easier to assign your failures to living during extraordinary times requiring extraordinary effort and luck, rather than to poor preparation, planning, and training.

Your time is no different than those who came before you, nor will it be much different for those who follow. The rate of change in human society hasn't varied much. What you use as your yardstick for change today differs from what you would use if you lived during the 12th century, but disruptions in the patterns of life (and therefore in business) come often and create opportunities essential to progress. Paradoxically, the great power of the human mind is that it incessantly seeks to find patterns in the chaos of life, many times finding patterns where none actually exist.

THE MYTH OF STABILITY AND THE REALITY OF CHANGE

The idea that life—and business—was somehow more stable in the past than it is today is a fallacy. Not only is it untrue, the fact is that the last 40 years of western experience has been *more* stable than most previous eras. But stability is not the normal state for human endeavor. So if it's been relatively quiet for two generations, you can bet that all hell's about to break loose. Statisticians would say we're about ready to revert to the norm. We're just not sure exactly when. We are sure when it happens everyone will claim that we live in extraordinary times.

The good news is that history shows that people are very, very good at adapting to change. Not that everyone will come out on top, but over time humans always re-discover how to thrive in a naturally chaotic world. What is important to you is how to ensure that you're one of the survivors. Several things separate the survivors from the failures. Many people fret that luck plays an unfair role in success and failure. As a recent western-movie bad-guy said (unforgivenly to his unfortunate victim before pulling the trigger), "Fairness ain't got nothin' to do with it." Luck by definition is available in equal proportions to all of us, but over time one thing stands out: Survivors capitalize on their luck by using their heads. Those who survive battle are known for "keeping their heads." Sure, some of us are going to get through on the back of Lady Luck. Others, even though they prepared themselves well, will be dealt a bad hand and get wasted. These are the exceptions.

The problem is not that exceptions occur, but that some people believe that exceptions represent the norm. A few people around them get undeservedly lucky. Others seem to be fortunate to have "natural" abilities to solve problems. Convinced that these are the only two modes of success, those temporarily out of luck either wait for a hot hand to rescue them or delude themselves into thinking that their natural abilities will somehow, someday kick in. For example, how many managers pay lip service to planning when they really believe that luck overwhelms all planning? How many managers depend on their "well-developed" ability to judge character but are barely functional in this area? How many have said that they are good negotiators, but can't explain the basics? Many people delude themselves into thinking that any success they have was a result of a skill they don't have and their failures a result of forces outside their control. In reality their successes and failures are outside of their control because they haven't tried to control them. They haven't taken the time to think about how the business world is put together. They see patterns where none exist and miss patterns where they are unmistakable, and they get constant doses of rationalization from the daily business press selling myths as fact.

THE THIRD FUNDAMENTAL SKILL

If change is the natural state of being, and if the historical record shows that those who respond to change wind up on top, then controlling the direction, pace, and impact of change must be a fundamental skill of general managers. The hackneyed saying that "Change is the only thing that stays the same" is meaningful, but only if you develop some sense about how all change occurs. In other words, change has a pattern. Once you see the common details of change, then you can do something purposeful when trying to get people to change in response to a changing environment.

THE THREE COMMON PHASES OF EFFECTIVE CHANGE

You could build a library of books written about the change process. However, what you really need is a simple model of how people change so that you can influence the direction and speed at which this naturally-occurring phenomena happens. In later chapters we'll discuss how the change model is applied to business problems. For now, we need to understand change dynamics in general.

People who study human behavior have identified three distinct phases necessary to modify behavior successfully: unfreezing, changing, and re-freezing. The first phase ***unfreezing*** is the most challenging one and demands most of your creativity as a leader. Unfreezing is the process of convincing those around you that staying with the status quo threatens their survival. The second phase ***changing*** is that amorphous state of change that always threatens to revert back to the status quo. It requires consistency, follow-through, and vigilance on your part. The last phase ***re-freezing*** provides a neat reference end-point. It is the marker that says the change is complete, that the sought-after modification has been completed. However, it is an invisible point in time. Since the group has accepted the changed state as the status quo, it cannot identify the day the change was complete. Re-freezing happens with few of the players seeing it. But the absence of re-freezing is always felt. If the altered behavior is not accepted as the status quo, you wind up with a disjointed group, some wanting change, others sliding back to the old habits. Most failures to re-freeze can be traced back to incomplete unfreezing.

Many fads built around controlling change emphasize technique over substance. They have elaborate management exercises, complex flow charts, and nifty jargon. In a later chapter we, too, will have our favorite techniques and tools. However, developing the ability to recognize the common phases of change is essential if you are going to use these tools effectively. Since each situation you face will offer different opportunities for change and will present resistance in different forms, you need to recognize opportunity and resistance. Eighty percent of controlling change requires this facility. The remaining twenty percent comes from how well you wield the tactical tools.

SPECIALISTS USE SPECIAL LANGUAGE

Before we explore the elements of each of the three phases of change, we need to clear up two things. First, we need to emphasize why this specialist language—unfreezing, changing, re-freezing and all of their accompanying terms such as disconfirming information, change agent, and force fields—is necessary. Second, we want to explore the first trap that you may fall into when you try out your new skills.

When you learn a new vocational skill, you expect to learn a new specialist language. Learning this lingo has several advantages. First, it makes it easier to communicate complex ideas to others who are also familiar with the terms. Second, it allows you to embody in a word or two previously unknown or unseen ideas. That is, jargon gives form to the formerly formless, potentially improving communication. Last, jargon identifies practitioners to each other.

There are many pitfalls to jargon, the most obvious is that many users never learn the deeper meaning of the concepts behind the words. Many of today's business fads—and change dynamics is surely one of them—are the consequence of superficial understanding of complex ideas. For instance, *change agent* is a term commonly used in change literature. Ostensibly, this agent is a person who guides, manages and otherwise controls the change process. But if you don't go beyond the introduction and build on your elemental knowledge, you'll always think that a change agent is a unique person occupying a special place in the group process. In fact, current business fad practitioners even offer courses that supposedly teach you to become a change agent, as if by assignment you, too, can be anointed. But as soon as you start using "change agent" as shorthand for this important protagonist, you shut yourself off from seeing a change agent as something other than an individual. A change agent is not necessarily embodied continuously in the same person, is very seldom appointed, and many times hard to identify. But because the word *agent* comes from our language of everyday use, the ordinary definition can overwhelm the special meaning.

For instance, in baseball one of the first things a promising young batter learns is to distinguish different fastballs. His task is made easier because all he sees when first learning batting skills are fastballs. Young pitchers can't throw much else with control, so they depend on "smoke" to get by batters. But as a batter matures, the word "fastball" takes on a more robust meaning. He no longer sees that blur he saw in his early years. He sees all of the nuances: the different pitchers' preparation, delivery, ball movement, placement, and speed. The jargon becomes more meaningful, not less. Unfortunately, in the business world many managers only get a superficial treatment of many of their survival skills, don't practice them incessantly like sports professionals do, and just use them to impress themselves. When used often, meaningfully, and with care, jargon plays a critical role in the learning of any complex skill.

THE FALLACY OF MANAGING CHANGE

While it seems that the first trap is falling victim to the Siren song of jargon, there's a more deadly one waiting for you. It's the idea that what you are doing is "controlling" change or "managing" change in others. It's easy to forget that you are the object of change, too. You can easily be seduced into assigning yourself the role of change agent. Many managers we've run into over the years will talk your ear off when describing how hard it is to change their people but fall silent when asked about how they go about changing themselves.

So when you put some of the ideas presented here to work, don't forget to put yourself into the picture. Refrain from appointing yourself as the change agent. You might have influence but not because of any appointment. If you don't participate in the change, those who work around you will see your efforts as nothing but managerial manipulation.

THE PARADOX OF FEAR AND SAFETY

All real change starts with overwhelming disconfirming information. No one is going to change the way they work, react, or otherwise think about a situation unless they are convinced that their current work, reaction, or thinking is hopelessly flawed, which is what disconfirming information does. Disconfirming information challenges your basic belief that things are okay. It's the information that says everything is *not* okay with your world.

For instance, why do you suppose advertising is so effective? Because it delivers the disconfirming message that your current behavior is somehow flawed. When you're being sold an inexpensive item, say a soft drink or beer, building disconfirming information is not much of a task for the advertiser because the cure to your "poor" behavior is immediately available and relatively painless. You can buy a sports drink and shoot hoops like Michael Jordan or Shaquille O'Neal, or you can buy the beer and hang with the beautiful people. Advertisers seek to change your behavior, and they often use disconfirming information to build fear and thereby motivate change.

The problem with relying on fear to motivate becomes obvious when the risks are larger than buying a beverage. The larger the risk a person is asked to take, the more obvious and overwhelming the disconfirming information must be. But to endure such psychic pain, you must have a safety net, a handy cure. Suppose we tell you that your industry will be essentially wiped out in five years, that industry employment will fall nearly 40 percent during that time, and that you'd better start looking for another line of work. (This is a real world example: the US domestic oil industry employment between 1984 and 1989.) Not only would the evidence have to be overwhelming for you to believe it, you'd have to convince yourself that the opportunities available in other industries are better than the perceived threat. In other words, for you to make such a large and risky change, you have to possess *psychological safety.* Otherwise, you'll build all sorts of specious arguments against any evidence for change we can bring you.

In their small world, advertisers bundle disconfirming information and psychological safety together. They tell you that you're a nerd, but hey, everyone else used to be just like you before they used the advertiser's product. They make it easy for you to identify yourself in the ad, and they make the solution seem effortless. This bundling of disconfirming information and safety shows up with a vengeance when sellers of fashionable business fads come to town.

This subtle paradox—that fear induced by disconfirming information can only motivate if it is accompanied by something that insulates the fearful—is why un-freezing is so difficult. The disconfirming evidence has to overwhelm because we are usually talking about significant change, but the vehicle for change has to be readily available to those who might feel threatened. This second element in the unfreezing phase of change, safety, is the one most managers cannot deliver unless they possess the six fundamental skills we introduced in Chapter 3. Why? Because when facing a true, overwhelming and undeniable need to change, people will look to their leadership for that safety. If the person in charge is confident and consistently delivers the goods, then those who look for that leadership will find the safety they need. We're not talking about leadership embolden by raw confidence. That's a given. More importantly, that confidence has to be reinforced with a successful track record that can only come from possessing sustainable core management skills.

RECOGNIZING UNFREEZING

At this point you know a few things that you can do to direct change, *whether or not your name appears in the "right" place on the organization chart.* If your view of an impending threat is to be taken seriously, you have to provide credible, constant information about the situation as you see it. You have to offer (1) a working hypothesis for change, (2) shelter for those who might be threatened, and (3) a way for them to move ahead. There is a true story told of a small group of men isolated and trapped on the beaches of Normandy in 1944. This band of survivors had been separated from their assigned units. All their officers and NCOs had been killed or wounded. Organized leadership and communications were obliterated. In the desperate huddle of men stalled on the beach, one rose to the occasion. Paraphrasing his words, he said that at the end of the day there were going to be only two types of people left on that beach—the ones who had already died and those who were going to—and he had no intention of joining them. He said he was going forward and anyone who wanted to live had no choice but to join him. While opportunities of such overwhelming fear, grave consequence, and obvious safety are unavailable to us in business, thank God, the lessons are available to us.

How can you tell if someone or some group is unfrozen? Simple. They begin to listen, and you don't need special training to know whether someone is listening or not. Unfortunately for those in the technology-will-replace-human-contact industry, you cannot tell if someone is listening unless you're in the same room. This is another reason change initiatives fail. The person who has the authority to commit funds relies on reports and second-person accounts, never seeking out those who are the "object" of the change. Without good, first-hand information about how the change is progressing, the responsible manager distributes rewards and punishment haphazardly, dooming the project.

One of the truisms about manufacturing is that not everything you need to know can be put on a print. The same can be said of this model of change. At this point you've been introduced to the three phases of change and been given some details about the first phase, unfreezing. But don't fall for the idea that this is a linear activity even though the model implies that it is. People don't reach an "unfrozen" state and stay there waiting for someone to come along and manipulate them into the second change phase. You have to continually paint and re-paint your landscapes entitled "The Failure of the Old View" and "The Triumph of the New". Otherwise, people will naturally slip back into the old state.

THE FALLACY OF EMPOWERMENT

Later in this book we'll look at different management fads in detail, but this is a good place to introduce a criticism about one in particular: empowerment. Many people believe that empowered subordinates can find their own self-defined problems and generate their own solutions. The premise is that people, given the green light by management and the right tools, are the best device to initiate, implement, and resolve change. Management's role is to get out of the way of this natural creative energy. By this time you must be convinced that while this sounds nice, change doesn't happen this way.

Change is a leadership responsibility. Lacking leadership, many targets of change will not be able to understand, relate to, nor care very much about the new attitudes, assumptions, or work necessary for change. Not that they actively resist changing, but without a unified vision they cannot sustain change. It is undeniable that the opportunity for change, the energy required to move forward, and the identification of alternatives can come from individual group members. But it is beyond comprehension that a business fad such as empowerment can assume that useful, profitable change will happen without intervention, without a plan, and without recognition of how people and their social groups actually change.

RE-FREEZING

Rather than discussing the middle change phase in any detail at this time, let's move to the last phase, *re-freezing*. The literature is full of advice on how to "manage" the actual change state. That phase is actually the shortest and easiest to work, given that you've learned the fundamental skills of management. We'll give you a few tools, such as free-form organization charts and force field analysis, to use during the change state later in this book, but for now they are just a distraction.

The most difficult concept to accept about change is that re-freezing is not something you do. We can identify activities to pursue in order to unfreeze a work group: collecting and sharing disconfirming information; identifying passive resisters; looking for opportunities to suggest safe passages to the future state. We can also identify activities that are helpful during the change process: revisiting the reason for the change; deciding how progress will be measured; drawing force fields to illustrate the forces working for and against the change; identifying players who are so disruptive that they have to be removed. But re-freezing is not an activity-based change phase. It exists in the collective minds of the players. For example, take the typical experience of smokers who successfully stop smoking. While they may be able to tell you the date they had their last cigarette, they won't be able to tell you the date they changed from an ex-smoker to a non-smoker. The day they stopped smoking was the start, not the end, of their effort to change. The end of the process is less recognizable. Nothing changed on that date, except everything.

APPRECIATING THE PROBLEM

A good way to appreciate how hard it is to change and what the different phases of change look and feel like is to try a controlled change experiment on yourself. First, pick some innocuous habit you want to change. Avoid the typical hard ones like losing weight, cutting back on alcohol, learning a foreign language, or appreciating your in-laws. Those change initiatives require so much disconfirming data and huge amounts of psychological safety that they rarely are done alone, nor completed in a short period of time, nor is the re-freezing phase very distinct. Instead choose something you'd like to do differently but won't take much more than motivating yourself—or so you think. Some typical, low-risk change initiatives we've seen include:

- Putting up everything in the family room before you go to bed
- Closing cabinet drawers and doors when you're finished with them
- Getting up when the alarm goes off—consistently
- Getting regular, low-stress exercise, like walking every day after work

- Asking for the manager each time you get poor service
- Taking time to read each day
- Generating a daily to-do list before you start your work for the day
- Starting every meeting with the word "profit"
- Taking notes during every business meeting no matter how short
- Ensuring that you talk to each one of your direct reports each day

Once you've chosen the change initiative you'll use to demonstrate the change process, keep a simple, single-entry-per-day, one-page diary about your attempts to change your behavior. It will be easier if you pick the same time of day to update your diary—before you leave work for home, before you retire to bed—so that you don't forget. Note that keeping a diary is a change in itself. Keep these notes for a month, longer if you want.

What you will find will be fairly typical. First, when you feel like backsliding, you'll question whether the change you want is so important anyway. You'll rationalize why on certain days you just couldn't work on your project. Many people will not be able to get through the first week of this challenge without giving up, which is okay. You need to know how hard it is to change behavior, even when the risks are minimal.

But if you are successful in changing some part of your life, even if it wasn't the change target you set for yourself at the beginning, you'll notice that a vital awareness developed during the change project. At some point you were able to sustain the change—re-freeze—because the value of the change became so apparent and overwhelming that you couldn't imagine going back to your old behavior. If during this forced march you fail to reach this state of awareness, you most likely will be unable to make the change permanent. If you changed a bad habit common to other people, too, you'll become more enthused and will want others to experience the change themselves.

This pseudo-religious conversion has implications for changes in your company. Any change worth doing involves the general manager or someone of similar stature in the group. Someone in the group has to get religion in order to generate enough energy to sustain the change initiative to the re-freezing phase. It helps if you see this happen within the context of your personal planned change so it will be easier to recognize it when you are working on group changes. In the end this little exercise is useful regardless how it turns out. If you fail, you'll understand how the model can identify the problems of directing change. If you succeed, you'll appreciate the intense satisfaction from working through a seemingly simple but ultimately complex change.

THE MYTH OF MODELS

A word of caution about business models: They are not reality, nor is their predictive output *in itself* very valuable. This is a significant distinction that will keep you out of untold mischief. We use models all the time in business. Your financial books, product design procedures, and sampling inspection programs all are models that simplify reality. The change model presented in this chapter is obviously a model of individual and group behavior.

One of the myths of models is that their predictive power is their predominate value. That power is an illusion. The real value of models is not in prediction but in diagnosis. For example, most engineers claim they can predict product performance and reliability, which is undoubtedly true. They send reports to management showcasing their sophisticated models and predicting a certain capability and capacity for a proposed product. What they leave out of their neat recollection of their design is how they actually used the model. They used it to diagnose a significant problem that emerged during product testing. Engineers are reluctant to admit that their models merely reflect test data and field performance. They'd rather believe that models are a testament to engineering finesse and creative insight. Not that engineers are dishonest; it's just that their dominate paradigm classifies the model's output as its predominate value.

The same should be said of the model of change dynamics. Like all models it should be classified as a diagnostic tool rather than a predictive one even though it does both. It's best used to figure out what the problem with your change initiative might be rather than forecasting where problems might occur. When a product unexpectedly fails during testing, engineers go back to their models to identify heretofore unrealized but now identifiable weaknesses. When a change initiative gets into trouble, you need to go back to your model of change and see where the problem might be. Prediction is fun and must to be done to set up the initial experiment. However, it is a mistake to miss the diagnostic value of models in preference to their predictive value. As you will see in later chapters, predictions on average, no matter what their source or apparent sophistication, seldom come true. When they do pan out, the predominate factor is luck although most owners of successful predictions will point to their superior but always proprietary model. Using models for predictive purposes is a parlor game. Diagnosis is much harder work, more emotionally intense, and abundantly rewarding because only diagnosis can be used to improve mediocre or failed performance.

7

Chapter 7

The Starting Line

In Chapter 6 we introduced a simple model explaining the basic elements of all change. It included three phases: unfreezing, changing, and re-freezing. While the model is useful for understanding change dynamics in general, you need to translate this general model into one that is more useful as a toe-hold on the mountain of problems you face in the real business world.

GOALS, OBJECTIVES—WHAT'S THE BIG DEAL?

Even before embarking on a change initiative, a general manager needs to answer two elemental questions: "Why change?" and "What are we going to change?" Finding satisfying answers to these questions is not as easy as it seems. Counter-intuitively, you should answer the second question "What?" before answering the first question "Why?" But the logic to this approach is inescapable. You won't know if a certain change should take place if you haven't adequately explained what you're going to change. Much like the scientist who first forms a hypothesis before building the experiment, you have to start with an idea of what you think needs to be changed before building your "experiment" to test whether the change is necessary. As it turns out, explaining what you think needs changing is actually easier than determining whether or not to change.

A common mistake is to answer what should change by stating goals rather than objectives. We regularly encounter managers who claim that an upcoming project will "break down barriers," "improve communications," "strengthen morale," "improve quality," "change the way we think," "help us become more entrepreneurial," or "empower people." While all of these change objectives regularly appear in the general business press, they are goals, not objectives.

Be clear on this: You cannot design a change project to achieve a goal. You have to translate goals into more concrete, measurable objectives. The difference is obvious when you try to define the project to the people who will be involved. For example, take the goal of improving communications. That's one you hear often after a train jumps its track. "We've got to improve communications so screw-ups like this don't happen," says the boss. The post-mortem meeting usually breaks up with renewed commitments to keep each other "more informed." A week later nothing has changed. When we say nothing has changed, we mean your work habits remain unchanged. You still hold the same meetings in the same way; you still issue and receive the same reports; you still report to the same person and the same people report to you; your daily routine continues unaffected. If you had stopped to say, "Keeping each other more informed is a good goal, but how are we going to achieve that?" you would have framed the right question. Your change initiative can now be explained in concrete terms. This is the only way you can develop alternative actions.

Incidentally, whether you intentionally do so or not, those alternatives will always be directed at changing the way work is done. Real change inevitably involves the *system*. In the case of trying to "improve communications", maybe you'll design more structured staff meetings; maybe you'll overhaul your nonconformance reporting system; maybe you'll change work assignments; maybe you'll re-design reports; maybe you'll re-assign people; maybe you'll institute more results-oriented training; maybe you'll hire someone; maybe you'll fire someone. In all cases your change objectives result in tangible changes to work routines.

CHANGING TO IMPROVE PROFITS VERSUS CHANGING TO IMPROVE LIFE

So it comes down to this: The objective of any change initiative in business is the method of work. In the trenches, change is not about improving communications, although better communications may result. It's not about improving quality of work life, although people may enjoy their work more. It's not about strengthening morale, although people may show more *esprit de corps*. Changing a business means changing how people do their daily work, which, in turn, may affect the way they look at their work and the people around them. However, that's a consequence of pursuing a change objective; it cannot be the objective itself. Changing work is how profits are increased and expenses reduced. If you have a change project with an objective to change anything other than work patterns or output, you're wasting money.

That is not to say that regularly scheduled sales indoctrination meetings, complete with pep talks from the vice president of sales and maybe an outside motivational speaker, is not a good change tool. However, such change activities have to be seen for what they are: training. What we have to remember but often forget is that such meetings must have an outward, measurable result, a change in the way work is actually performed, which results in increased profitability. If these activities don't yield measurable results, then the change initiative is an illusion where activity displaces achievement.

In summary, the objective of any change project in your firm has to be a change in the way people in your organization do their work. All other outputs are irrelevant.

WHO SAYS WE HAVE TO CHANGE ANYWAY?

Unfreezing is a phase that really overlays the change phase. The best way to test if you've begun to thaw out is to ask, "Why change?" This question has to be asked often and answered vigorously. In the beginning it is fairly easy to answer the question "Why?" with a list of compelling reasons. As more information about the actual change becomes available, the risks and rewards are better defined. As you pursue your objective, you reach a point of maximum doubt about whether the project is viable. One of the most debilitating management tendencies is to invest time, effort, and money in change initiatives that are premature or simply not appropriate for the company. The result is a never-ending parade of new change initiatives, started with fanfare and deep commitment only to die a slow, unnoticed death.

In the beginning of an anticipated change initiative, the reason for changing may be easy to state, and the answer to "Why change?" is treated as obvious. But only after you generate alternative action plans can you appreciate the number of people involved, which ingrained habits will have to be changed, who and how many people are aligned against the change, and how much safety can be constructed for those who will be affected. Only after you've answered the question "What are we going to change?" are you in any shape to answer the question "Why change?" in any cogent way.

Because the order of these two start-up questions actually occurs out of "natural" order, many general managers get caught up in change initiatives that should have been killed. It's difficult to stop a process with a question you've already answered or one that was treated as obvious. It's not a question you would generally ask unless you appreciate that unfreezing is a management activity that has to be continuously applied throughout the change initiative.

WHAT DOES "YES" SOUND LIKE?

As with most real life questions, your answer to "Is this change necessary?" becomes more equivocal, tentative, and conditional the more you ponder it. How do you know whether you should proceed with the change project, knowing that the answer to the most critical question will be, for the most part, wishy-washy? There are several obvious signs. First, while your answer always becomes more tentative and conditional over time, the conditionality should become more concrete and manageable, and your anxiety about the project's righteousness should decrease. If you don't see this trend, you probably should abandon the change project. Second, even if you classify the change as mission critical, you may find that the action items are hopelessly incompatible with the assets you've got. In that case you have to abandon the project.

Canceling a project is as important an activity as proclaiming a new one. It demands that the company leadership be very honest about what is possible and what is not. In some cases the desirable change is beyond the capability and capacity of the firm, in which case the original change project may have to be abandoned in favor of a more fundamental change.

For example, suppose that you want to design and install a documented standards-based management system in your company. You've decided that if you don't, your overhead and rework costs will continue to grow. Your survival in an increasingly price-competitive market is threatened unless you get a handle on these costs. This is a mission-critical project. As time goes on, you realize that you have had little success convincing your staff this project holds the salvation of the company. Worse, you realize that you yourself are having trouble adjusting to emerging price competition in a market that has been, until now, more focused on product features than price. The longer you attempt to make a change that neither you nor your staff feel compelled to do, the less time you have for developing alternatives that may work better for both everyone. There are other genuine, understandable and supportable reasons for canceling a change initiative. What was first seen as critical becomes less so when given more information. Priorities change. Other opportunities present themselves, and given limited budgets and personnel, you may find it necessary to shift to other work.

KILL IT BEFORE IT DIES OF NEGLECT

Companies abandon mission-critical projects all the time. It's just that their management usually avoids public burials because they are more concerned with saving face than saving money. Instead of presiding over a very public burial, most hope the failed projects will just fade away. After a while, these managers ensure a self-fulfilling prophesy. Their disregarded programs do seem to fade away. But what they don't realize is that these programs don't fade away; they become another profit-eating ghost roaming their halls. Over time, the office and plant will be full of the walking dead. Management pretends not to see these zombies, or worse, they see them but hope no one else does.

Why do these projects turn into ghosts rather than just die of neglect? First, if you don't give them a public burial, people will generate their own epitaphs. For example, some will say management is so unsure of themselves they cannot admit to a mistake; others will be more charitable and say that the project was a mistake. Of course, attempting a change is never a mistake; not giving it a necessary burial is. Since you didn't take the time to explain to those who worked on it why it had to be abandoned, your neglect turns what was a good fight into an limp-wristed fuss.

The second danger in avoiding public burials is that people will begin to disregard and even avoid all new projects. They begin to see these projects as a manifestation of management ego rather than real attempts to solve real problems. These ghosts wander the halls adding more fuel to the fire of office rumors and innuendo.

Last, without a clear signal that a cherished project has been canceled, some people will continue to work on it way beyond the time they should. Instead, they proudly generate valueless work. Just because you assign new work or tacitly encourage them to return to their old work without clearly rescinding the previous objectives, some people will not see this as a clear signal. In fact, within any group of people attempting a change, there will be those who, for various reasons, will want to hang onto the project until the bitter end. It's the first time in a long time they think they've had something worth contributing. But the longer you put off the inevitable, the worse they are going to feel about the cancellation of their favorite work.

SOLVING THE PROBLEM

You undoubtedly have several ongoing change initiatives at your work. Whether or not you see yourself as responsible for them, write down what you believe their work objectives are. Ask the question, "Are these changes necessary?" Write down the various reasons you believe that the projects should continue. Put the paper away for six weeks.

In six weeks, look at what you wrote. Compare your thoughts six weeks ago with what you believe today. Have these projects really moved forward? Are they more or less pressing than they were before? Have new ones replaced old ones? Have any been completed? Have any been put out of their misery? Look at the entire collection of change initiatives within your company, not just your pet project. Do they really result in change, or are they just change for change's sake?

Another benefit from this little test is realizing the power of paper and pencil (or the computer equivalent). We are not talking about generating memos or E-mail on a whim. We're talking about reducing ideas to paper as a craft. Too many companies either don't write enough down or write too much of the wrong thing. The most important management information you can write is an explanation of your decisions. This historical information is critical to good management because it allows you to re-visit decisions without depending on your memory. While your mind is without equal, the astonishing thing about it is how unreliable your memory is. If you are paid for the output of your grey matter, the most important thing to remember is that you don't remember.

For example, have you ever gotten in an argument with your significant other where both of you were adamant that your recollection of a shared event was the right one but each was 180 degrees opposite. Not only are the recollections different, but both of you earnestly believe the other is totally and unmistakably wrong. The fact is both of you are telling the truth. This is why crime eye-witnesses are notorious for giving conflicting accounts of what they saw even when they are standing next to each other. The power of the mind to synthesize coherent pictures of life from small bits of recalled information is what gives the mind its power but is also the source of self-delusion in business. The bottom line, on the other hand, rarely forgets.

What you need to do is prove to yourself that not only do projects become the walking dead but that your recollection of the facts and circumstances surrounding their past is very unreliable. With that proof behind you, you'll appreciate the need to keep track of every change project using a planned and documented record. That record will give you the undeniable information you need to cancel some programs and encourage others. Without the facts, you live a fantasy, and while fantasies are fun, they seldom are profitable.

8

Chapter 8

The Finish Line

The reasons for the high failure rate of corporate change initiatives are conspicuous and demonstrable. Remedies are harder to come by. We have to change the way we envision, devise, and implement planned change. The second of the three distinct change phases—the implementation or transition phase—is complex. Each initiative has its own personality driven by the peculiarities of your company and the people involved. Nonetheless the high failure rates imply the existence of a common set of remedies. So far we have discussed the things you need to do in the early phases of a company project. Now, we look at the things you need to do to improve the chances that your process for change stays on track during the long, hot summer of change, when new ideas seem worn and everyone gets a little drowsy.

But before we get to the nuts and bolts of managing the transition phase, we need to emphasize that the change skills outlined here are good for all kinds of change projects, not just the latest business fad. Not only are "new" company-wide change initiatives like Total Quality Management (TQM) failing at unacceptable rates, the failure rates of all "special" projects are inherently high. Recently we attended an industry forum of software engineers concerned with out-of-control software development budgets and resulting mediocre product performance. Different speakers repeatedly quoted widely-accepted failure rates of 70 percent in their industry—a failure rate strikingly familiar to professionals involved in high-profile corporate quality initiatives. The audience listed familiar reasons for failure: vague and constantly changing objectives, under-estimating the resources and time required, inadequately trained personnel, and the ever-common "poor communications." This last cause triggered someone to mention the problem of technically-challenged management. Snickers filled the room, then embarrassment. All of these reasons were generated within three minutes and, in some form or another and to some greater or lesser degree, are common to failure of every botched change initiative. This commonality across industries and professions strongly suggests that responsible management lacks a basic understanding of how to keep projects on track and how to help people stay focused while implementing change, regardless of the technical disciplines involved.

THE USUAL TOOLS

If you've had any experience running large or complex projects, you're undoubtedly familiar with Gantt charts and similar project management tools. But if you haven't had the opportunity to use these charts and techniques, don't worry. You're in the majority. While they are widely taught and in many cases invaluable when managing some projects, we are more interested in what they *cannot* do rather than what they can do. Like so many management tools, knowing how a tool like Gantt charts can be misused is as important as knowing how they are used.

For those who need a reminder, Gantt charts (sometimes called time lines), are named for the man who popularized them. They visually represent the project's tasks, the tasks' relationships with each other, and the projected and actual start and completion dates (see Figure 8.1). Their sophistication and versatility make them indispensable for managing complex, detail-driven projects, such

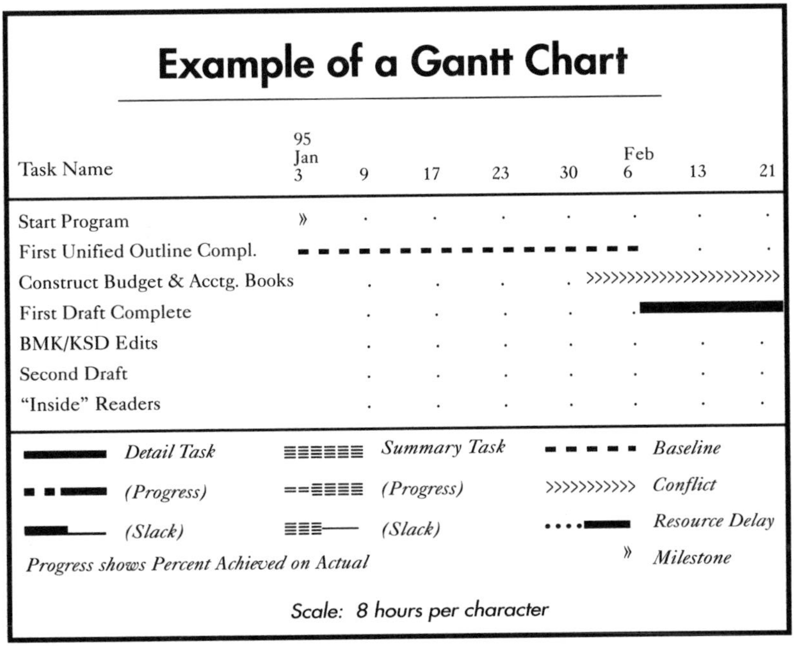

Example of a Gantt Chart

Task Name	95 Jan 3	9	17	23	30	Feb 6	13	21
Start Program	»	.	.	.	.	.	.	.
First Unified Outline Compl.	▬ ▬ ▬	▬ ▬ ▬	▬ ▬ ▬	▬ ▬ ▬	▬ ▬ ▬	▬ ▬	.	.
Construct Budget & Acctg. Books		.	.	.	.	>>>>>>>>>>	>>>>>>>>>>	>>>>>>>>
First Draft Complete		.	.	.	.	.▬▬▬	▬▬▬	▬▬▬
BMK/KSD Edits		.	.	.	.	.	.	.
Second Draft		.	.	.	.	.	.	.
"Inside" Readers		.	.	.	.	.	.	.

▬▬▬ *Detail Task* ≡≡≡≡≡≡ *Summary Task* ▬ ▬ ▬ ▬ ▬ *Baseline*

▬ ▬ ▬▬ *(Progress)* ==≡≡≡≡ *(Progress)* >>>>>>>>>>> *Conflict*

▬▬— *(Slack)* ≡≡≡— *(Slack)* ••••▬▬ *Resource Delay*

Progress shows Percent Achieved on Actual » *Milestone*

Scale: 8 hours per character

Figure 8.1

as commercial building construction and civil improvements. With the advent of PC-based project management software, Gantt charts can now be used to model and track smaller projects, such as new product development or plant extensions, cost-effectively. While project management tools are usually associated with activities that have physical outputs, like a building or product, they are frequently used to control company-wide change initiatives, such as reengineering and TQM as well.

The difficultly in using a time line to represent project progress is that *process* can be mistaken for *progress*. For instance, let's say you decide to install a documented standards-based management system like ISO 9000 or your industry's Good Manufacturing Practices (GMP). Your project goal seems easy to state: "To obtain second- or third-party certification of our documented system." Early in your planning cycle you reduce all of the necessary action items to various tasks, assign responsibility, estimate required time, and use a canned computer program to determine the critical path and relationships between the various tasks and the estimated completion date. You use the resulting Gantt chart as an early warning tool, allowing you to determine where you are diverging from your initial plan or conversely how wrong your initial plan was.

In Chapter 6 we cautioned against using models solely for their predictive power and neglecting their diagnostic power. The same must be said of Gantt charts. It's easy to appreciate their predictive power. After all, if a certain task takes longer than the time allotted, most PC-driven Gantt charts will automatically predict how this early-stage problem will affect subsequent tasks and how far the finish date will move. Commonly overlooked is what these cascading adjustments imply about project health. Unfortunately Gantt charts are not issued with a warning stating: "The root cause of changes needs to be investigated." Instead, the ease at which you can make changes to these charts insinuates that scheduling problems are routine and schedules flexible. While any particular scheduling problem *might* be routine, repetitive re-scheduling indicates that the original assumptions concerning allocated resources and costs are suspect, or that the project is headed in the wrong direction, or that some other of the many common and systemic problems associated with planned change projects may exist.

This is another instance where a model intended to illustrate deviance from original intentions becomes a pseudo-predictive model. What is forgotten in the thrill of the newly accessible technology is that the original schedule was a best-guess, and therefore what later passes for prediction remains a guess. This type of misuse of models can be avoided if you train yourself to be less enthralled with their predictive powers and instead more appreciative of their diagnostic value.

Before we leave Gantt charts we should emphasize that they, like all pseudo-predictive models, are good tools and do indeed have their place. They will unfailingly tell you the impact of lagging tasks on the whole program, assuming that the rest of the program follows your original best-guess. In recurring programs, like building a highway or dam, institutional memory is a great asset. In these circumstances Gantt charts are good tools to ensure that tomorrow's project leaders can capitalize on today's lessons. However, while their predictive power is central, obvious, and improves with repeated use when applied on the same repetitive project, their diagnostic power, unfamiliar to many, can be applied to non-repetitive projects. Therefore diagnosis is the predominate value of any model when you are facing systemic problems like the overwhelming failure rate of corporate change initiatives. While you might find that a Gantt model is necessary to track all of the interrelated tasks of a complex change initiative, this is seldom sufficient to ensure that projects stay on course. Even though they show progress against plan and imply where root causes might be hiding, they cannot illustrate the state of more fundamental problems like resistance, relationships, and momentum. You need a different set of project tools to illustrate the current state of change and reinforce critical change behavior.

THE UNUSUAL TOOLS

If Gantt charts are nice but over-rated project management tools for the kinds of projects in which we're interested, what's left to help us manage change? Up to now we have emphasized the need to define your change objectives in terms of work output, the importance of regularly revisiting the necessity for change, and the value of recognizing the three distinct phases of change. We've explored the first phase, unfreezing, at length because it is so essential to successful change. We mentioned that the third phase, re-freezing, is merely an end-point that we usually note in passing. The second phase of change—the transition itself—remains to be explored. While many change projects fail because of insufficient and incomplete unfreezing, others fail because we cannot sustain the energy level and awareness required to see the project through to the end. The following tools will help you overcome what we know are the typical reasons change initiatives fail during the transition phase:

- ***Understanding the Gestalt Cycle of Experience***
  The Gestalt Cycle of Experience is a surprisingly practical way of understanding the role awareness plays in change. By appreciating this seemingly simple behavioral model, you'll understand how awareness and focus might be influenced, how to keep on track, and, more importantly, how to help other people avoid the inevitable dissipation of attention.

- ***Running meetings***
  While it's very trendy to avoid meetings because they have become superfluous, significant change projects cannot sustain themselves without meetings. Meetings *are* superfluous time-wasters because managers don't know the basic elements of good meeting stewardship.

- ***Using free-form organization charts***
  Free-form organization charts help illustrate how work actually gets done. Realizing the nature of the organization behind the organization is essential for removing or reducing barriers to change.

- ***Applying force-field analysis***
  Force-field analysis is a handy way of illustrating which forces help and which hinder change. Most project breakthroughs occur when forces opposing change are removed rather than when supporting forces are invigorated.

- ***Measuring change***
  In business, if you can't measure it, it doesn't exist.

HEY, PAY ATTENTION TO ME WHEN I'M TALKING

According to our dictionary, ***awareness*** is having or showing realization, perception, or knowledge and "implies vigilance in observing or alertness in drawing inferences from what one experiences." All of us are aware that we are aware. We also are aware that other people's awareness differs from ours. Even so, we know that we can affect the awareness of others because we do it every day.

Suppose you get on a subway, and the person sitting next to you lights up a cigarette, contrary to the "No Smoking" signs. You mention to her that smoking is not allowed on the train. She promptly has a snit and calls you various uncharitable names. The next thing you know everyone is razzing your neighbor about her cigarette. She puts it out and mumbles a few choice good-byes to you on her way out of the car.

Let's analyze what happened. It is very likely if you had not said anything about her behavior, no one else in the car would have spoken up, either because they weren't bothered or they didn't want to bother. By speaking up you brought their awareness of a particular issue—rudeness—into their mental foregrounds. Apparently many in the car, once you brought the issue up, realized that they really didn't care for the smoker's rude behavior either. At this point it is easy to believe that your fellow riders were waiting for someone else to say something. While some may have been, most were not. In a car of 30 or 40 people the chances that perfect strangers are reacting to their environment the way you are is very, very slim. People get lost in their own very personal mental foregrounds and backgrounds. Some are tired and content to daydream. They don't want to interact at all. Some are looking forward to meeting their family or friends. Some are still struggling with a problem back at work. Some are not feeling well and are concentrating on their discomfort. Once you brought up your issue, their mental foreground was disrupted, but each one still had his own personal and specific reaction to the situation. That the crowd's intensity equaled yours once its collective awareness caught up to yours was just coincidence. Another time and place they would have left you and your new friend to settle your differences.

This feature of our self-referential world—that our perceived world (and therefore the business world at large) exists only in the mental foregrounds and backgrounds of individual people—is a powerful tool for understanding how groups lose focus on change objectives and how you can get them back on track.

What we have described in the preceding example is a layman's application of the Gestalt Cycle of Experience to group dynamics. You probably use fragments of this model without realizing its origins. Have you ever said, or heard it said, that you have gotten (or reached) "closure", meaning that you have reached a consensus among different parties about a common issue and that each person was preparing to move on? *Closure* is part of the jargon of Gestalt psychologists, but many who use the term are unaware that they are borrowing from this field of study. Furthermore, Gestaltists say that closure also represents learning, meaning that the actors have extracted the meaning from the common experience.

Figure 8.2 is a simple illustration of the cycle for a single person while Figure 8.3 represents the cycle for two people engaged in a common activity. These representations are far from being technically rigorous. We've left out many details, simplified definitions, and mixed various levels so that we can extract the central value of this model for you: Successful communication of and action toward any goal requires that all parties reach peak action states at the same time. It helps when the intensity of action is equal among the parties, but a lack of intensity is not as counterproductive as people reaching the action plateau at different times, that is to say, be "off-cycle", like it is in Figure 8.3. These two people will have a hard time moving the project ahead because they are seldom "on the same wavelength". When one is ready for action, the other is not. This inevitably leads to each believing the other has no interest in the project, when in fact they both do, but at different times and at different intensities.

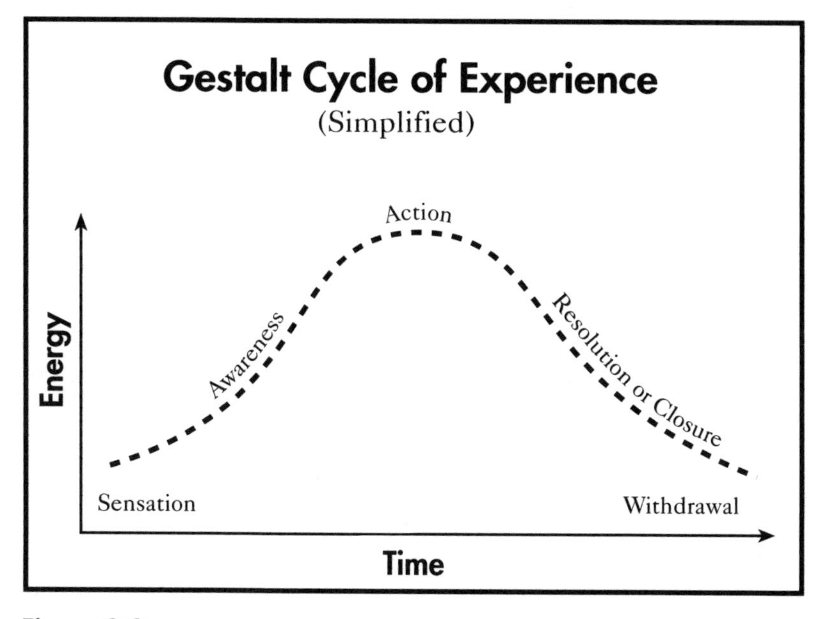

Figure 8.2

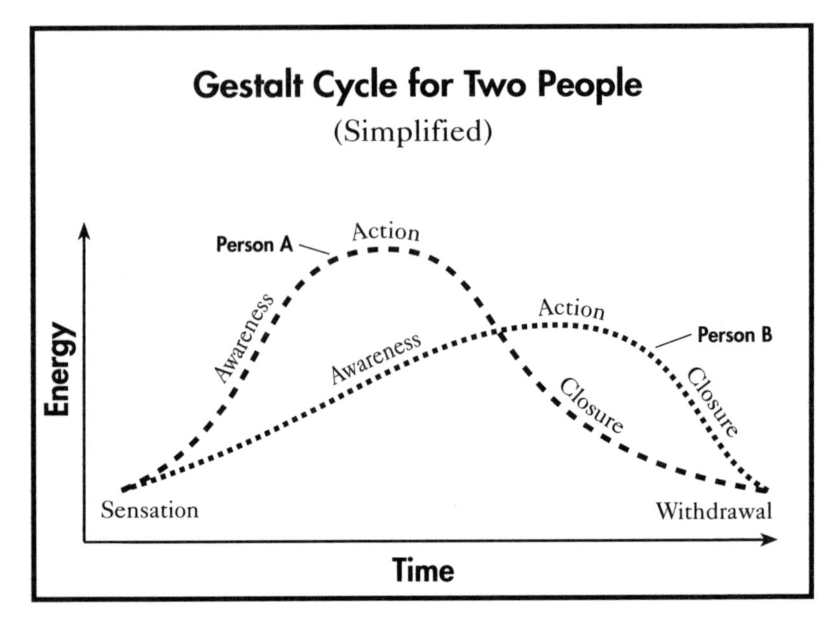

Figure 8.3

The speed at which a project can be completed is related to how long the action phase can be sustained or how often the cycle repeats. If the two people in Figure 8.3 remain off-cycle, they may still get something done together if the cycle repeats itself often enough.

The action phase cannot be sustained indefinitely; closure has to occur in order to build understanding necessary to start the next action phase. If people don't get closure often enough, they get tense and dissatisfied with their progress. Everyone has to take time to look back at their experience before moving forward. If they are forced to move forward before they get closure, all of the open issues crowd their foreground.

Change initiatives that become dysfunctional during the transition phase almost always do so because the responsible leader lacks an appreciation of his role as the instigator and supporter of the phases preceding and following action, i.e. awareness and closure. While all the phases of the

Gestalt Cycle are personal and internal activities, awareness and closure are the two where an adroit leader can be most affective. Some leaders have learned one-half of the lesson and are known for "keeping the pressure on". Their success with change is higher than most, but they would be more successful, and less disruptive, if they spent an equal amount of time on the closure needs of their people.

This simple model of interaction, although a complete and indivisible cycle, is centered around awareness. The issue of awareness is something we encounter every day yet hardly reflect upon. Not only is the Gestalt Cycle a helpful tool for diagnosing project implementation problems, but also it is extremely valuable for organizing your own thoughts about your personal problems with self-motivation. Awareness is the essence of the transition state. Only if you as the leader can *see* how you can affect individual awareness during the transition state can you bring energy to bear on the obstacles to change.

Let's look at a small change project. Say you want to teach your dog to retrieve a frisbee. First, you have to build the dog's interest. Some dogs are not going to have a problem with this. Anything you're interested in, they're interested in. But suppose your pup is more discriminating. She enjoys playing with your old sock but not a frisbee. Unfortunately for quick progress, you want her to fetch frisbees. She just sits, looking at you play with that flat plastic pan and thinks (like so many other things you do) that you've lost your mind. Then one day she starts showing interest in your frisbee. The next day, she backslides. Nothing short of sticking it in her face makes her the least bit intrigued. But she always has that old sock. At this point, you have to either decide if you'll be happy playing with her favorite sock or if you want to continue building interest in the frisbee. You know that given enough time and patience, she will learn that the frisbee is your preferred toy.

The point of our little parable is not that people are like dogs, but that if you want to reach your objective, you need to constantly monitor and reinforce awareness levels during change initiatives, both *your* awareness as well as others'. A particular problem with many managers entering the transition state is that they fail to realize that they alone are responsible for monitoring awareness. Too often people know that they can passively resist a change just by ignoring it. They know that the boss historically shows only episodic interest in these types of projects. With brief, sharp awareness/action peaks and long lulls between cycles, they know that they can doom the change project. The critical factor for project leaders is that their own awareness has to precede awareness in others.

In the example of training your dog, changing over to playing with a sock is no big deal if your goal was to enjoy your pooch. However, if your goal was to train a champion free-style frisbee dog, you might retire your current dog to the country and get yourself another dog. Changing your objective to sock-playing in the middle of the project is okay, as long as you do that consciously. You've only replaced one project with another in light of the resources and energy available. But if you change it because you let your foreground picture fade due to neglect, you no longer have a project; you have a problem. Similarly in business, if you start program after program as a reaction to letting what is foreground and background change without thought, then your company will be dysfunctional.

Now that you are aware of awareness, how do you ensure that awareness remains high and projects move forward? The core implementation activity that boosts awareness is well-run meetings.

CLOSE ENCOUNTERS OF THE PROFITABLE KIND

Our dictionary defines ***to meet*** both as "to encounter" and "to come together with, especially at a particular time and place". Similarly, we are interested in both the short, two-person chance encounter in the hall as well as the typical conference-style meeting where people gather to discuss pre-determined issues. In both circumstances at least one participant is attempting to influence the awareness of others. In the realm of change initiatives, these meetings focus people's attention on the on-going transition phase.

Speaking of dogs, meetings are dogs if they fail to bring the group to common levels of awareness or if they fail to reinforce closure for all participants. Even though meetings seem to be universally disliked, they are the best tool for reinforcing common goals and ensuring that ideas are thoroughly debated and communicated. A physical meeting with all the players is one of only a few forums where the leader is seen as leading the group, as opposed to interacting with individual players. Finally, face-to-face meetings have a human dynamic which is difficult to replace with networked, technologically-supported intercourse available through E-mail or groupware.

This last point deserves exploration. For our purposes a *virtual meeting* supported by network software (also called groupware) is a meeting even if the sense of time and space is abstract. Groupware is attractive technology because it controls meeting costs by reducing the frequency of face-to-face meetings, just as well-written and judiciously circulated memos or well-organized telephone calls do. This technology also seems to create new ways of interacting and affects interpersonal relationships in ways classical meeting formats cannot. However, in our rush to take advantage of this new technology, we forget that relationships developed through physical human contact are unavailable from groupware-supported communications. Successful change initiatives require that the actors as a *group* reach similar activity plateaus often and simultaneously in real time. This basic function of physical meetings is problematic for groupware-driven formats. The extent that new technologies like groupware help or hinder the Gestalt Cycle will ultimately determine if these technologies are useful. Whether or not new technology will make face-to-face meetings redundant is a fun cocktail-hour or health-club topic, but it's immaterial to the job of encouraging change in people. What is important is that the combination of meeting and communication technologies used by the group doesn't inadvertently neglect group awareness needs.

THE CHANCE ENCOUNTER

If you are responsible for a project, you must ensure that awareness levels are regularly and vigorously stimulated and that closure and withdrawal is closely followed by additional sensation (see Figure 8.2). If you are a general manager, you may have several significant on-going change efforts and will be concerned with the awareness of different and sometimes overlapping groups. You, of course, would not have "too many" projects. If you did, you would be violating the principle of unfreezing that indicates that there is a practical limit to the number of changes that can be supported by sufficient and credible disconfirming information.

The only way you are going to be able to keep these initiatives on track is to take every opportunity to boost periodically the awareness both in yourself and in others participating in the change. Regular, written reminders coming out of your office or E-mail is fine, but nothing is as powerful as personal presence. Every chance encounter you have with subordinates and peers should include a recollection of the project, even if it is a quick recitation. Additionally the Gestalt Cycle indicates that even chance encounters follow the cycle's distinct phases.

Poor person-to-person communication starts with an assumption that the person to whom you're talking has the same foreground figure as you do. That is seldom the case. For example, suppose you start a chance encounter in the hall with "Hey, Barbara, what's going on with the project?" You shouldn't be surprised if all you get is a blank stare. Barbara has no way of knowing what information you need. She will try to form a figure from her background and hope it matches yours. On the other hand, it is better to start your conversation with a picture of your foreground: "Barbara, I've been reviewing the latest project report and notice that Bill may be having trouble. Tell me what's going on." Barbara's awareness rises rapidly to meet yours. If, on the other hand, you've not done any work on the project in some time, you could start your question with a statement like "Barbara, I haven't yet looked at the project reports, but I'd like your assessment of where we are." In either case Barbara doesn't have to guess what your foreground figure might be. It's not coincidental that reporters usually preface their questions with a statement. It gives their target a better chance of answering the question that follows.

Some managers believe if they telegraph what's on their minds, they won't be able to ask open-ended questions that help uncover what is really going on. They miss our point. It is not that you can't ask open-ended, undirected questions. It is that *if you want to use your time efficiently* you have to let the other person know the lay of the land. Otherwise, what passes for good, probing give-and-take is nothing but flailing around for common mental ground.

For example, suppose Girard runs into his occasional acquaintance Marie on the street and asks, "Are you doing anything tomorrow night?" Up to this point their relationship has been limited to small talk and a quick lunch with mutual friends. Having presence of mind, she will hesitate to answer until she knows why he needs to know. There will be much hemming and hawing, probing, misdirection, and general uneasiness. Maybe Girard likes undefined, tension-filled conversations. However, if he doesn't (and most of us don't), Girard is better off if he starts his question by laying some groundwork. Suppose something she says makes him think she might be looking for something to do. Instead of asking the whatcha-doing-tomorrow-night, open-ended question, he ought to say something like, "A couple of us from work are going to the ballgame tomorrow night. Do you want to come?" That tells Marie everything she needs to know about the question. On the other hand, suppose he has a different impulse. He instead says, "Jenny and I just broke up. Are you doing anything tomorrow night?" Marie has a different picture of Girard's foreground. Whatever is on his mind is unknowable until he tells her. Any question put to her comes bundled within context. By prefacing his question with what's on his mind he has a better chance of a clean communication. Of course, Girard may not know what is on his mind or may know that he is ambivalent about the situation, in which case he should be prepared for an awkward encounter.

Awkward encounters in business always cost money and should be avoided. Honesty within the company or group pays dividends, so say what's on your mind first, and be sure that before closure you've asked about the state of change in your on-going initiative. We, of course, are excluding activities outside of the group where competitive negotiating suggests that revealing what's on your mind can cost you money.

Besides framing questions so that they convey your foreground figure, all of your chance encounters should in some way address the on-going change project. If you allow these brief meetings to drift over the landscape and conclude without exploring the change project, you've lost an opportunity to reinforce the transition state and display your leadership interest in the objective. Even if it is only a parting line like "Don't forget we have a meeting on

Monday to review our work progress on the LMNOP project," you have provided a small boost in the person's awareness. What he does with that increased awareness is immaterial in the short-run, but over the long-run such constant, incessant reminders work magic.

THE PLANNED MEETING

There are various types of planned meetings. Without making precise distinctions between the different kinds of meetings, let's observe one interesting truth. Regularly scheduled meetings, like weekly sales or production meetings, seem to be better run than *ad hoc* meetings used to run special projects. This implies that if we want to make project meetings more productive, they should include the features of regularly planned meetings. These features include the following:

- ***Clear Objective***
  An ***objective*** is "something toward which effort is directed." Before meeting participants gather, they should know the precise expected outcome of the meeting. The objective statement must be clear and unequivocal. A "better understanding of our problems" might be the purpose of a meeting. In fact, such a statement reflects the role of meetings in adjusting the awareness of participants; however, it is not an appropriate meeting objective. Examples of well-stated objectives include "review of and concurrence with proposed Action Item list," "discussion of current project status reports," "generation of ideas for Product XYZ's locking feature," and "review and sign-off on Nonconformance Reports." These meeting objectives allow better preparation by giving participants an idea of what the meeting is supposed to accomplish and how to prepare for

it. Meetings may lead to better understanding of collective problems, but saying a meeting's objective is "better understanding" is a non-starter. It's a little like your friend telling you to get ready to go out tonight without telling you if you're going to a drag race or to the opera. The goal is to have an enjoyable time; the objective is the means by which you plan to do so. Without knowing the objective you won't know whether to wear your comfortable clothes or your finest threads.

- ***Time Management***
  Not only do the most productive meetings begin on time, they also end on time. *Ad hoc* meetings are a bit more difficult to plan because you're guessing how long closure will take. Regardless whether or not you got through your agenda, you *must insist* that these meetings end at the assigned time. If you have to stop short, it's obvious that the meeting's objective was too broad. Under this circumstance, it's always better to withdraw and reflect, even if it is only for a few hours, so that the next meeting can be better focused and controlled. A rule of thumb we follow is that *ad hoc* meetings held on site should be limited to 1½ hours. Keeping people's awareness on the task at hand for longer than that is difficult when other competing work is just outside of the meeting door.

- ***Agenda and Participant Selection***
  Most good meetings are driven by written agendas. The regular weekly production meeting runs off a production form or data sheet. Likewise, project meetings need written agendas, too. Agendas take the meeting objective and break it into manageable, logically-progressive activities. Also,

writing an agenda makes you decide who needs to be in the meeting, what data is required and who will bring it, and what order issues and information will be presented.

- ***Action and Closure***
  As the Gestalt Cycle implies, anytime awareness increases to the degree that a foreground figure emerges, it generates energy for action. Furthermore, closure concerning the meeting gives participants both a sense of accomplishment for the time they spent away from their "regular" work and a clear sense of what has been decided. The action phase of project meetings invariably extracts work commitments from various people. This commitment generates tension within participants that is only released when they complete their commitment and get personal closure, thereby moving the project forward. Of course, if their commitment was only verbal and not psychological, they will leave the meeting with no intention of honoring their commitment and essentially have personal closure the minute they walk out of the meeting. As far as closure is concerned, people get something out of meetings if they see them as learning experiences. To ensure that participants leave with a feeling of accomplishment, the leader should provide formal closure. A recitation of the commitments and decisions of the group is absolutely required. Setting the time of subsequent meetings helps, too. Merely mentioning that the participants will be notified later of the next meeting is sufficient.

These elements address the structure and maintenance of meetings. Other features of good meetings, such as how to conduct them, interpersonal elements, and good agenda-writing techniques, are covered in references provided in the appendix. We believe that if we insist that every *ad hoc* meeting have a written objective and agenda and that every project meeting conclude with some written output, project leaders will be able to both generate hard, tactical value as well as reinforce the collective awareness necessary to keep change projects on track.

FREE-FORM ORGANIZATION CHARTS

Another tool for moving change projects forward is the free-form organization chart. The limitations of formal command-and-control org charts (Figure 8.4) are so frustrating that many companies refuse to draw any. Free-form org charts shown in Figure 8.5 (also called activity-based org charts) were developed to overcome the rigidity of formal org charts by limiting their illustration to relationships between people when they are working on a particular process and by using various techniques to reflect the different types of relationships. While not a substitute for conventional org charts, free-form org charts provide relational insights on how work is done.

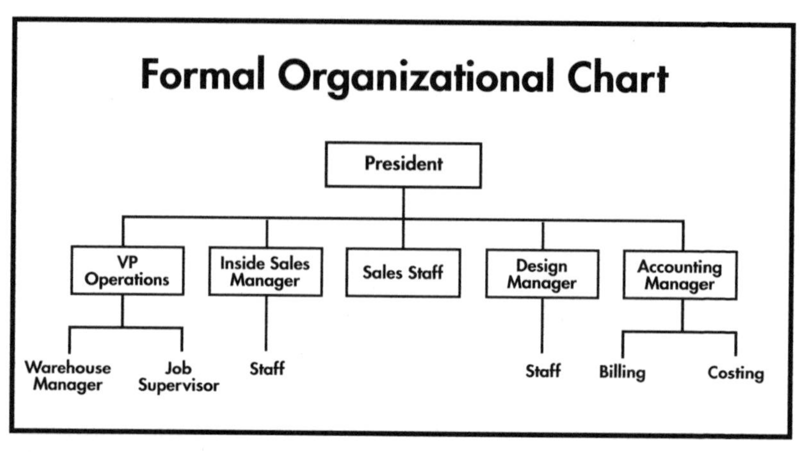

Figure 8.4

The recent disreputation of formal org charts is an example of how poor application can lead to rejection of a perfectly good tool. Believing org charts are commonly misused and therefore are useless for illustrating relationships is as silly as believing that keys are useless for opening doors since they are also used to pry open paint can lids. More to the point, the disfavor of org charts says more about the impact of recent management fads emphasizing "open" organization structures than it does about the real limitations of formal org charts.

It is true that the familiar organization chart rarely reflects true working relationships. However, org charts are supposed to model the performance-responsibility chain, not necessarily working relationships. It's not surprising that they rarely show how actual work is done because they were never intended to do so. Those organizations that depend on org charts—the military comes to mind—know that these charts have a very narrow and spe-

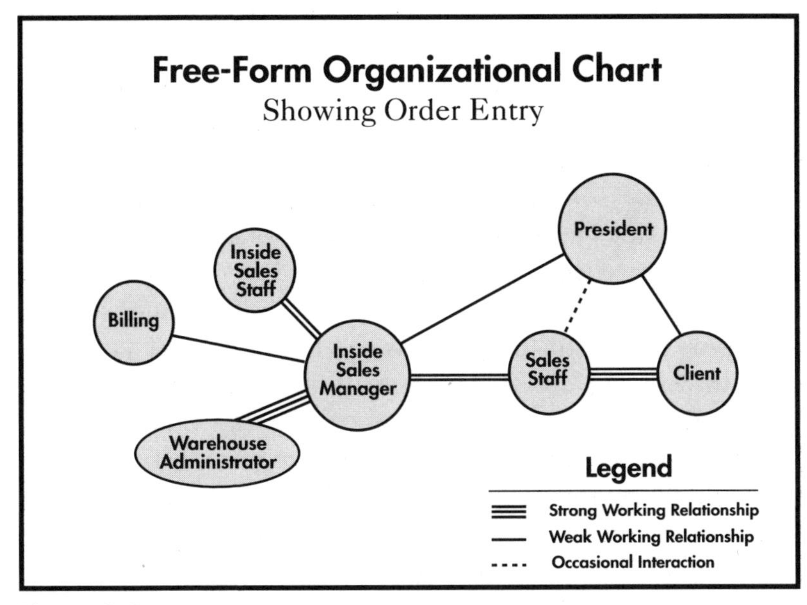

Figure 8.5

cific use. They need these charts because their kind of work requires that each person know, beyond any doubt, who is responsible for his personal direction, well-being, and sustenance. In fact, all businesses need to answer these basic questions, but people aren't killed if these questions are ignored.

Organizations that rely on formal org charts know very well that the informal organization is where most of the real work gets done. For instance, org charts seldom show technical relationships. A machinist may report to the shift foreman for his work assignment, as the org chart shows, but he may rely on a senior craftsman for set-up assistance and on the president for material performance expertise. The org charts says nothing of these relationships. The org chart may show the quality assurance manager reporting to the president when, in fact, he sees himself working for the plant manager. Few organization charts have arrows showing where the customer enters the picture, although that interface is a critical feature of the company's control systems. These working relationships vary over time and depend on the activity being investigated.

When embarking on a change initiative you should model the informal organization using a free-form org chart. It will help you see who has a stake in the changes and whose participation is essential. Suppose you are going to reduce the number of steps and hold points in your order entry system. While you trace the path of a typical order from customer call to work order issue, you will come up with a list of people who play a role in the process. At the center of your org chart draw a circle with the name of the predominate person involved in the process. As you draw other circles representing other actors, you may decide that not one but several people occupy the center of the activity, and therefore you might place several near the center. As for representing the relationship between people, you could signify a strong working relationship by two solid lines, a weaker relationship with one line, and an occasional interaction by a dashed line. Some people like to use distance from the center to represent influence on the process, but that can make drawing the chart more difficult.

When you finish your free-form, you will see relationships that are impossible or inappropriate to show on the formal org chart. You will have a better idea at what point and with whom the customer interacts. Realizing the nature of the organization behind the organization is essential for identifying who can influence the direction of the change you want to implement.

Refer back to the free-form org chart in Figure 8.5. This is an example pulled from our files. Several relationships are evident on this org chart that were transparent on the formal org chart in Figure 8.4. First, the free-form chart only applied to the order entry process, not the entire organization or all of the processes. Second, the president's link to the sales people was a weak one even though the formal organization chart shows them reporting directly to him. The sales personnel had a stronger relationship with the inside sales manager than they did with the president, but only as far as the order entry process was concerned. Third, the client rarely, if ever, interacted with inside sales, which in this company served more as sales support than anything else. Next, the inside sales staff interacted almost exclusively with their supervisor, not with the outside sales staff or customer. Last, there was a strong relationship between the warehouse administrator and inside sales manager. The administrator didn't even show on the formal organization chart. During interviews it became apparent that the inside sales manager developed an informal relationship with the warehouse so that she could get vital information on scheduling and stock levels unavailable through the formal organization. The formal organization chart reflected none of these working relationships, but then it was never intended to do so.

Another use of free-form org charts is for general diagnosis of the current state of work relationships. At the beginning of a major change initiative involving the entire company, the project leader should sit with the major players individually and draw a free-form org chart with the interviewee at the center of the chart. Instead of focusing on a specific function, you'll be asking each person to think about his working relationships in general. Say you have six key people. You will wind up with six free-forms. If there are significant differences between these charts because certain people see strong or weak relationships where their counterparts see the opposite, then you have radically different perceptions of how work is accomplished. If your change project depends on these relationships for success, you'll need to address these misperceptions directly before you can proceed with the transition phase of your change project.

FORCE-FIELD ANALYSIS

Another popular tool used to illustrate the dynamics of change is the force-field. A simple tool, the force-field shows the forces aligned with and opposed to change. This information is invaluable for maintaining change momentum since it allows you to determine what opposing forces must be removed, as well as which supporting forces might be helpful. Removing opposition turns out to be more critical than enhancing supporting forces. This is similar to salespeople knowing that they must identify, address, and isolate all objections before they can close a sale. To change a company you have to sell an idea first.

Figure 8.6 is a free-form diagram for the change initiative associated with the order entry project example mentioned earlier. The line down the center of the diagram represents the present state that must be metaphorically moved to the right. The items on the left are the forces for change, those on the right oppose change. The size or num-

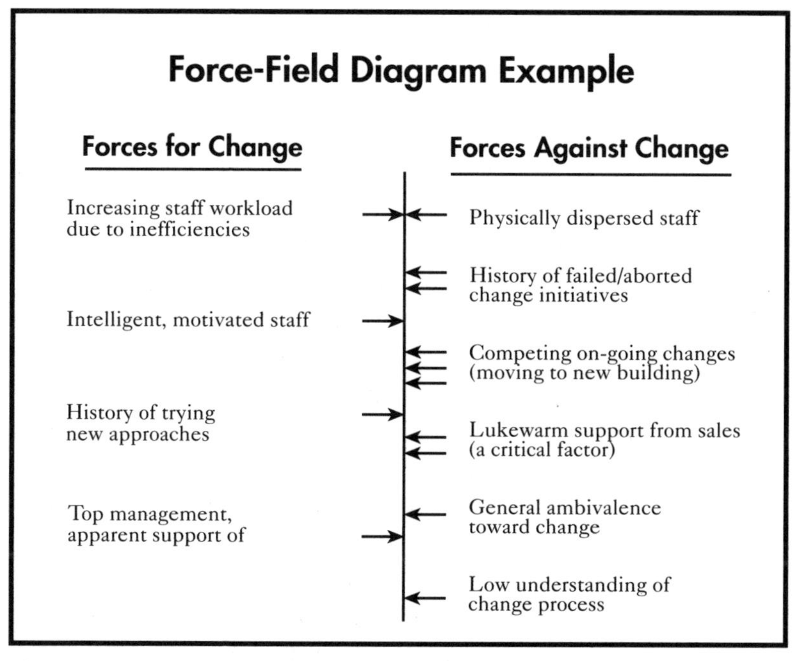

Figure 8.6

ber of the arrows associated with a force indicates its relative strength to the other forces. In most instances you'll be able to come up with more opposing than supporting forces.

In this real-life example we identified three opposing forces that had to be removed if we were to have any chance of seeing the project to its conclusion. First, in six months the company was scheduled to move from dispersed operations around the city to one central location. We questioned whether it could endure such a disruptive change and still remain focused on this relatively small but important project. The president decided that they would merely suspend work on the order entry system during the most intense activity period associated with the move. Second, the company had a history of starting change initiatives and letting them dissipate. None had been successful. We were concerned that this history of failure would color people's enthusiasm towards this latest change project. This was a distributed opposing force, not centered in an individual, and could only be overcome by deed. Third, during the early part of the project it became evident that the sales department representative—a critical actor in the change effort—had little interest in the change. She was uncomfortable with her central role, had little training in or understanding of systems analysis, and perceived few rewards for her efforts. The president was aware of this but saw the project as one which could also help this staff person overcome her shortcomings.

Not surprisingly this project failed, too. The move to a new location was inadequately planned, exhausted the staff, and, because of cost overruns, left the company with less financial breathing room. The move also introduced tremendous amounts of disconfirming information about all phases of the operation, not just order entry, and thereby overwhelmed management. Unfortunately, this avalanche of bad news disoriented rather than focused the president and his staff. The planned change gave way to unplanned fire-fighting.

That the force-field diagram "predicted" this outcome is immaterial. What is important is that those involved in the change effort identified the opposing forces accurately and addressed them as best they could. Without the benefit of generating the force-field, discussing the significance of the forces aligned against the project, and addressing these forces prior to the undertaking, the project had *no* chance of success going-in. During the formal closure phase of the project (which incidentally never happened), a review of the opposing forces and their role in the failure of the program would have reinforced the idea that the probability for success was directly related to these known forces.

MEASURING CHANGE

Just because you can't measure something doesn't mean it doesn't exist. Love, hate, beauty, quality, goodness and evil all exist even though we cannot objectively measure them. On the other hand, in the circumscribed world of business and profit, you must believe that *if you can't measure it, it doesn't exist.* This fact, and the frustration that goes along with it, plays havoc on rational people. In a 1995 headline article in *CFO* magazine, financial leaders of companies such as General Electric, IBM, AT&T and Pepsico relied on hyperbole to express the financial success of reengineering. Such was their total detachment from reality that some were quoted saying that most of the benefits of reengineering were unmeasurable, but nonetheless they believed reengineering was a resounding success. It's a sad day when the Kings of Quantitative Rationalism run out of creative ways of illustrating the value of a significant and costly undertaking like reengineering.

Let's re-state the maxim: If you can't measure it, it doesn't exist. How about "If you can't measure it, don't bother with it?" If you believe that programs like reengineering defy measurement, don't undertake them. If someone else in another company can measure a program's benefit, it is not a poor reflection on your company that you can't. It indicates that either you lack the understanding of the program's costs and benefits and therefore shouldn't undertake it until these costs and benefits become more evident, or if you do understand it, you shouldn't undertake it because it holds insufficient benefits for you. On the other hand, maybe those competitors or friends undertaking the latest fad management program are in such poor condition compared to you that they can get value from it even if you can't. Or maybe they are in such poor condition that they have no idea that their profitability model is bogus. In any case, your mother was right. Just because your friends are jumping off the Brooklyn Bridge, why should you?

Of the different skills required to get a program through the implementation/transition phase, figuring out what to measure and how to value it requires most of your creative and quantitative skills. You should be concerned with two numbers. First, assuming the project will be completed, what will be the cost and monetary benefits? Second, what will you measure to show that the project had its intended effect?

Following our example of improving the order entry cycle time, its cost is mostly opportunity costs, mostly your people's time. Instead of working on this project, they could be working on another. So before you start the project, you must estimate how much time will be required for the staff to do the analysis, write the new procedures, test them, train employees, and implement the new work rules. A good rule of thumb, if you don't have a track record for estimating the work load for these types of projects, is to try to think of all the steps involved, estimate the time required, and double it. Now you have an estimate of how much time and money this project will cost.

Ignoring opportunity costs is the first place people go wrong. Some will say that the project is cost-free since the people working on the project are already on staff. This reasoning concludes that since salaries are within reason a fixed cost, the project is free. Nothing in life is free. Even if this staff is salaried, all incremental work they perform costs the company real money. Opportunity costs are costs associated with doing one thing rather than something else, and they are real. The fact that you cannot imagine what they would be doing if this project did not come along results from limited imagination, not from limited work opportunities. If you indeed had no inventory of profitable project work, you soon would realize you are over-staffed.

Back to our example of reducing the order entry cycle time. Suppose you figure it will cost $25,000 to get all the way through the program. Now you have to quantify the benefit. Some will say that it is obvious from inspection that reducing order-entry cycle time is a profitable venture and spending time on quantifying the benefit is a waste of time. Not so. Look at the ways you could *increase* costs when you decrease order-entry cycle time. Suppose you have no hypothesis on how reducing order-entry cycle time will reduce overall cycle time. Furthermore, suppose the project staff determines that the only way you are going to decrease order-entry cycle time is by hiring more order-entry help because "everyone is loaded." You've just added structural costs without showing how it will be paid for, much less how it will make you money. Alternatively, you may streamline the number of order-entry review steps, thus freeing staff from this function, but find out later that the cycle time in the plant can't take advantage of faster order cycle times. If the freed staff time is absorbed by assigning it to lower-value, nonessential activities, you've just rearranged the cost structure and have yet to make any money from the costly changes.

If, on the other hand, you hypothesize that your study will free up staff time while overall cycle time remains the same, then before you invest in the study itself you must plan how the excess staff time will be used. Either employees will be put to work on higher value activities resulting from company growth or be eliminated from the balance sheet. Suppose you believe that reduced order-entry cycle time will result in a reduction in overall cycle time. Then, you have to translate that hypothesis into a plan for utilizing the increased capacity by increasing sales. When sales increase concurrently with a reduction in order entry cycle time, the marginal profit on the additional sales increases because you don't have to add staff to take care of the increased sales. However, if sales don't increase and you decrease cycle times (thereby increasing capacity), you have no return for your improvement project.

These various ways of looking at a "simple" project illustrate how important it is to have a concrete concept of how your project will generate marginal profit. Without this concept you may have a successful program—i.e., reducing cycle time—but receive no benefit from it. The discipline required to generate hard numbers also forces the planning staff to answer hard questions before the project is underway. If your going-in hypothesis is that a project will result in a staff reduction, certain consequences are implied. If the hypothesis is that it will result in additional capacity, different consequences are implied. The accuracy of the calculation is not as important as your plan to capitalize on the change.

A favorite example of spending money on a pet project without showing a return is the currently popular customer questionnaire. Some of today's faddish quality programs imply that to be a "world-class" company you have to have a program of regular customer surveys. Quality departments regularly insist that they need surveys because "everyone" has one. Besides, customer surveys are a "cost of doing business" that cannot be justified on a current income basis. Not so. This is how the cost/benefit argument could be structured: First, someone calculates how much the survey will cost, then doubles it. Next, realize that the benefit from any data program, whether it be a customer survey or a plant data system, is not the data itself but what you do with it. In the example of a customer survey, you have to ask yourself what the data will allow you to do or what costs it will help you avoid. If all you do is generate numbers indicating how your customers "feel" about you with no working hypothesis of how that information will be used, you've just spent money on a survey without any resulting benefit. If, on the other hand, you design the survey to help you decide your next product improvement or prioritize your work, then the cost of the survey is rolled into the cost of the anticipated actions you will take based on the information you gather. The root problem with so-called "cost-of-doing-business" activities is that no one has taken the time to understand how the company can make money with them. Without going through the exercise, it is easy to add the cost and forget to plan how to generate value from it.

While telling stories of how project costs can be rationalized is easy, most of the time it's hard for you to translate them into your particular situation. As a manager you need a few basic back-of-the-envelope steps to apply to any proposed project. If you work for a larger company you may already have a standard format for pencil-whipping a project into a shape presentable to your investment board. Nevertheless, what separates the good project from a wish list is the character of the analysis, not the neatness of the presentation. So whatever incremental improvement project you run into and no matter its size, apply the following measurement elements:

- ***Generate a written estimate of costs.***
  Remember nothing is free, and remember to double your cost estimate. Even if you overestimate the cost, any project worth doing can support a doubling of its costs without jeopardizing its success. If you are presenting the numbers for someone else's approval, don't double the number, but show in your back-up that the costs may double without jeopardizing the project.

- ***Establish how the improvement will generate profit.***
  Don't forget if you squeeze costs out of a system, those costs have to be physically removed. Otherwise, it's just funny money. If you increase

capacity, remember that you have to have a plan for loading that capacity. Otherwise, it's just dead, excess capacity.

- ***Determine how these costs will be tracked.***
  How will you know how much a project costs you if you don't have a way of tracking expenses? If you don't currently have a project-centered cost system, simple daily time sheets showing how much time someone worked on the project will be enough. You're not trying to split the atom, you're just interested in measuring cost within a reasonable error.

- ***Decide which project activity measurement reflects progress.***
  Many corporate-wide and departmental improvement projects involve increasing the efficiency of work, especially overhead functions. While an investment in plant and equipment generates obvious progress indicators (e.g. "The pad has been poured, the machine set, and now we're testing"), measuring progress on projects aimed at increasing efficiency is a challenge. Whatever the activity, you've got to decide how you will be able to measure the impact of the project on the work activity. Many measurement schemes used to track improvement programs show progress even though most people involved agree that they've generated a lot of heat but little light. How many teams you've established, how many procedures you've written, or how many plants you've toured is no indication of project progress or completion. If your objective is reducing cycle time, then you have to measure cycle time to have any chance of knowing whether your project is mak-

ing progress toward the objective. If your project is decreasing rework, then you have to have a good system to measure rework. The fact that you've trained 83 percent of shop personnel in statistical process control is irrelevant.

- ***Ensure that adequate baseline information is available.***
  Many projects begin without the benefit of knowing baseline performance. Take time to generate that data before you start your journey. For example, if you are attempting to reduce scrap, how good is your current baseline information? Is your current scrap report accurate? Is it sufficiently precise to measure any improvement you might make? If the baseline information is solely anecdotal, then you have to spend time on setting up your information sources before you proceed. You might think this will hold your start time back, but if you have poor data, you probably have other opposing forces on the force-field diagram that need attention before launch time.

- ***Ensure that measurement methodology is in place and reportable.***
  If your information system was in place and generating good baseline information before the project started, ensuring that you will continue getting relevant data is not too difficult. However, if you had to set up new measurement methodologies, remember that you have to schedule time for training people and testing measurement reliability before you turn your attention to other details.

- ***Issue a financial analysis at the end of the project.*** If you're the owner of a company and ran the project yourself, maybe you don't need to document the project's success or failure. You've been intimately involved throughout the project and know what the numbers say. But if you are spending someone else's money, you should write a summary report showing the results of the program. This won't take much time if you've kept up with all of the other program measurement activities. If you haven't, you can only *claim* that the project was successful, you can't *prove* it.

GENERATING OPPORTUNITY

That completes our recitation of some of the tools you'll need to organize a change project. Our assumption up to this point has been that you've already selected the appropriate change project. But where do the ideas and opportunities for change come from?

In Chapter 3 we said that peculiar to the role of the manager is his responsibility to operate *on* the system. This requires that at times you as a manager have to go outside the system to be able to work on it creatively. One key can be found in the lesson of the Gestalt Cycle. In the rough parlance of Gestaltists, you have to practice suppressing your natural habit of forming figures from background noise if you want to free yourself from automatic thinking. By doing that, you'll see more change opportunities than you would be able to otherwise.

How do you do this? First, using the Gestalt cycle is a conscious activity, not the result of some mysterious Eastern enlightenment. You have to practice self-awareness. Try a little experiment. The next time you tour your domain—let's say your department or the shop—do so *without* an agenda. That is to say, go out to the shop or tour your department with an agenda of not having an agenda. Do a lot of listening. As soon as you see yourself forming a familiar foreground picture, drop it. Instead, pay attention to details you've never paid attention to before. You'll find yourself noticing things you've grown used to, such as peeling wallpaper, drafty rooms or poor lighting. Maybe you'll sense tension and disillusionment. Perhaps you'll be impressed by the intensity and focus. Whatever the case, you'll see artifacts you haven't seen before. More importantly, do not go back to your station deciding to address some issue you just dug up. Just let it go. This will frustrate you beyond belief because you haven't allowed yourself to form foreground figures about what you saw nor will you get closure. Later, when you are working on previously identified problems and applying the principles of planned change, something left over from your unfocused wanderings will float to the surface and have more meaning than if you had tried to force an issue to the surface at the time you observed the artifact.

Several years ago a management fad called *Management By Wandering Around* (MBWA) became popular through the book *In Search of Excellence.* Scads of managers eloped to the shop floor or to ground zero of their departments to try their hand at unfocused, undirected management. But like all passing business fads, the technique was oversold and poorly applied. It is extremely difficult work and requires strict discipline on the part of managers to refuse to draw an inference from what they see. Most of these new MBWA converts did nothing of the sort. They went out to the floor with an agenda. They allowed themselves to get caught up in a fire-fight. While they might have felt refreshed when they got back to their station, they missed the point. In the end, the fad was blamed for all sorts of company disruptions, which were inevitable because the management was not sufficiently unfrozen and ready to change their style. There was no overwhelming threat to energize them. They failed to prepare themselves with responsible training, and they mistook their goal ("We need to improve our management style") as their objective. Like all fads, MBWA started with good intentions but was perverted by managers who lacked the fundamental skills of management.

9

Chapter 9

Systematic Change

At this point you've gained an appreciation of why it is so hard to initiate, sustain, and complete change. You've even got a handle on how to identify profitable change objectives and test whether you're making headway. But some opportunities for change present themselves almost every day. You can't react to low-level disconfirming information in an *ad hoc* way. You have to have a rational way to process these opportunities. Otherwise, disconfirming information boiling up from below will either go unnoticed or create a management team with a firefighter mentality. That's not a healthy way to run a company. You need a system that anticipates potential sources of disconfirming information, categorizes them, and has planned responses depending on your own criteria. But how do you do that?

CONTROLLED VERSUS UNCONTROLLED CHANGES

To understand the variety of changes companies struggle with every day, you need to divide the world of change along two dimensions. The first dimension classifies the change according to whether the predominate source of the disconfirming information is *internal* or *external.* The second dimension determines whether the change activity is, or should be, controlled or uncontrolled. A controlled change is one that is guided by well-defined (and hopefully) written procedures or activities. Uncontrolled changes are those that go on every day without the benefit of systematic awareness. Some refer to uncontrolled change as *naturally-occurring change.*

One key to a successful change policy is ensuring that all change opportunities are put in the right class. If you put too many change opportunities into the controlled change arena, then you will overload management and stifle front line personnel. If you put too many change opportunities into the uncontrolled arena, then you'll be overwhelmed by suboptimum solutions and long-term dysfunction. While an overbalance in either direction leads to declining profitability, most American management teams today tend to put their faith in the liberating world of uncontrolled change.

To understand the consequence of inappropriate reliance on uncontrolled change, let's look at some real life stories of lost opportunity. In the first story, Bubba is responsible for moving semi-finished product from station-to-station for a company that designs and builds large processing vessels, the kind that have to be transported horizontally on flatbed trucks, by train, or on barges. One day Bubba gets a move ticket telling him to move a newly-built shell from the welding shop to the head joining shop. Bubba takes his crew over to the welding shop. They soon realize that the fabrication drawing didn't include lift eyes. This has been happening quite a bit lately. The first few times they ran into this problem, the production foreman told Bubba to have a welding crew tack on some lift eyes. So Bubba does the same thing this time. Two months later the completed tower rips the bottom off a highway underpass when a lift eye doesn't quite clear.

Bubba's change process relied on internally-generated disconfirming information and was uncontrolled. Bubba found that the method for moving material was consistently unreliable. It had to be changed in order for him to do his job more efficiently. To solve his problem he initiated an unplanned and therefore uncontrolled change. He took responsibility for attaching lift eyes when they weren't available.

These types of uncontrolled changes occur all the time in business. People are continuously subjected to internal and external disconfirming information that demand attention and resolution. These problems won't go away unless they are addressed—billing problems, payment problems, inspection problems, equipment problems, sales problems, every type of problem that has to be solved in order for the company to move forward, to complete a sale. Uncontrolled, naturally-occurring changes are those which people make "naturally". Over time people learn which problems are considered their domain and which must be left to others. Seldom are the boundaries of these domains described formally because there is no formal, recognized process for reviewing disconfirming information, generating creative alternatives, or communicating proposed solutions to people who work at the boundaries of decisions. These uncontrolled change domains can exist totally within one person's job or can involve people in several departments. The missing ingredient is that formal (i.e. written) change procedures are not engaged when they are appropriate to the problem at hand.

In Bubba's case he was given the responsibility for doing a job. He did it the best he knew how with the best intentions. In fact, he had faced the problem of lift eyes so often that he changed his work routine. He now was ordering out welding work. No one seemed to mind. In fact, the foreman was happy that Bubba was showing initiative. The weakness in the system is that Bubba had no way of communicating the need for a systemic change, no tools to direct the change itself, nor any method for analyzing the potential affects of his solution. When the vessel got wedged underneath the overpass, Bubba was the one left holding the bag. Maybe the final inspection person caught some heat, too. However, it is not Bubba's job to care and feed the system that ensures controlled change kicks in at the appropriate time, nor is it the foreman's. It is the general manager's, the person who is supposed to manage the boundaries between functions and build the company's business systems. Unfortunately many general managers ignore this dimension of their job because they don't have a clue how to direct systematic change—a fundamental management skill.

IT'S NOT ALWAYS BUBBA

Management always likes to point to Bubba as an example of how things can get screwed up, not realizing that Bubba seldom is the problem. Management is solely responsible for Bubba's predicament. But another true life example will show that management regularly reacts to disconfirming information with uncontrolled change, too, in situations that absolutely demand controlled change.

Irving was recently recruited by the chairman of a *Fortune 500* company to head one of their manufacturing subsidiaries. About three months into his tenure Irving gets a call from the chairman. "Bud", the chairman says, forgetting Irving's name. "I've just been talking to Lynn (another division manager) at the Triple D division. They've come up with a great idea to save money on their manifolds. They've reduced the number of weld passes and really increased throughput." Irving realizes he has to get with the program. His disconfirming information comes from an external source and is not so easily ignored. The information is loud and clear: "Irving, you're not doing your job as well as your peers. Show some initiative." The disconfirmation is more pointed since the chairman has already forgotten his name. Irving is the kind of guy who doesn't need as much psychological safety as some people. He got his job by being hard driving, taking risks, and generally bulling through any problem that got in his way. By God, he's going to make some changes around here.

Irving thunders down to the production line, talks to the welding foreman, and tells him to make the changes that the Triple D division made. Sure enough, after they make the change, overall throughput soars. That's where the production bottleneck was. Irving is more than eager to share his triumph with the chairman, especially because he was able to make the change so quickly. He might not have seen the opportunity as soon as his peers, but once on the job he gets it done NOW!

This story has two possible endings, but telling the actual result would spoil it. In the first ending manifolds begin to fail at a higher rate than before. In fact, the trend is not recognized for a year or so. It seems they've developed a nasty habit of blowing up in the field when the equipment they serve malfunctions. Of course, it took at least a year for anyone in the company to accept the externally-generated disconfirmation ("Your manifolds are failing . . . ") and then it only got the attention of the sales organization. After all, as far as the engineers knew, nothing changed. Why should their manifolds be failing? The last time they thought they had a problem they found out that those crazy customers were misusing them. Everyone seemed satisfied with the answer, except the customer. Time marched on, and Irving's manifold sales started to drop. "Just a bad market," everyone said. And that was true, the market was shrinking. Unfortunately for Irving, the excuse of a declining market masked the effects of the uncontrolled change Irving made a year before. When the market did revive two years later, Irving's manifolds didn't. Triple D's did. Eventually, Irving's division was sold off. One of the first things the new owners did was increase the number of weld passes.

You see, while the Triple D division was building the same manifolds that Irving was, Triple D sold them into a less demanding market. Triple D could lower the shock-design safety factor without any negative consequences.

Their manifolds never saw service anywhere near their nameplate performance. But Irving's division sold these manifolds into markets that operated them near their design limits. Irving's replacement called for the engineers to perform a full-blown failure analysis. They quickly discovered the problem but couldn't explain how such a design change could have been implemented without verification and validation reviews. No one left over from the previous regime could remember how the change was made since there weren't any records. The lesson remained unlearned.

The second possible ending to this story starts back on the same day Irving directs his uncontrolled change. Engineer Robb is wandering the shop floor the same afternoon Irving told the welding foreman to change the design. But Robb doesn't witness the directive. Instead, he notices that the pipe fitters aren't preparing the material as they usually do. He does a little digging. When he gets to the welding foreman, he finds out that Irving ordered the change. He tries to get the foreman to rescind the change since Robb realizes that the manifold's capacity to withstand shock load has been compromised. The foreman says there's no way he is going to tell Irving. So Robb decides to call Irving directly and let him know the consequences of his uncontrolled change. Irving rescinds his change, but for two years Robb's career goes nowhere.

Irving acted with the best intentions on external disconfirming information by forcing through an uncontrolled change, same as Bubba. The difference is that Irving should have known better. He knew the type of change he wanted to make is typically addressed by a systematic and planned change process. Furthermore, anyone familiar with manufacturing knows that production facilities are organized to anticipate design changes and that a well-run shop has systems in place that exclusively handle the type of change he unilaterally imposed. Bubba was only doing his job; Irving was derelict in his.

GOING OUTSIDE THE SYSTEM

Irving's reaction to disconfirming information is typical of many managers who have expensive control systems already in place. They ignore them. They think that these systems are too burdensome for men-of-action like them. Besides they don't have time to learn them. They've got things to do. Heaven help the person who orders a pencil without going through channels, but if the boss wants to buy a 10-million dollar building, he needn't follow protocol. He's empowered. He can get things done. "The guy who had this job before me is not here, so he must have been doing things wrong," he thinks. "I'm going to make some changes." The reason policy and procedure books fall into disuse is not because workers ignore them, it's because management does. Because they have the raw power to affect uncontrolled change with far reaching effects, they do so to the detriment of the whole company.

THE LONG TERM EFFECT OF RELYING ON UNPLANNED, NATURAL CHANGES

Over time companies like Irving and Bubba's go bankrupt in spite of the best intentions of their people. Figure 9.1 shows three stages of a business cycle. During the first stage the company is enjoying a certain level of activity. We'll assume that it's profitable. Behind the scenes there is a set of problems, represented by the companion bar labelled "C", that are held in check by uncontrolled, naturally-occurring changes put into place by the people who do the real work at Bubba's company. These problems are solved episodically. Some solutions are better than others, but the company manages to get by. Unfortunately, the inefficiency resulting from this problem-solving mode is hidden by the continuing profitability of the company. Lucky for them, their competitors' approach to running their own businesses is about the same. As problems come up, the management empowers the lower levels to work them out as they see fit.

During the second stage of the business cycle, company sales increase rapidly. Maybe the market is good; maybe the company develops a competitive product advantage. In any case bank debt is increased so that production facilities can be added. More people are hired to handle the increasing number of problems inherent in growth. Profitability is maintained. There's an uneasy feeling that the marginal profit on the increased sales should be higher than it is, but, for the most part, people are satisfied with performance. Behind the financial numbers is a policy of solving problems by relying on uncontrolled, natural-occurring changes. Management rarely gets involved in problem solving. After all, they believe they hire "good" people to

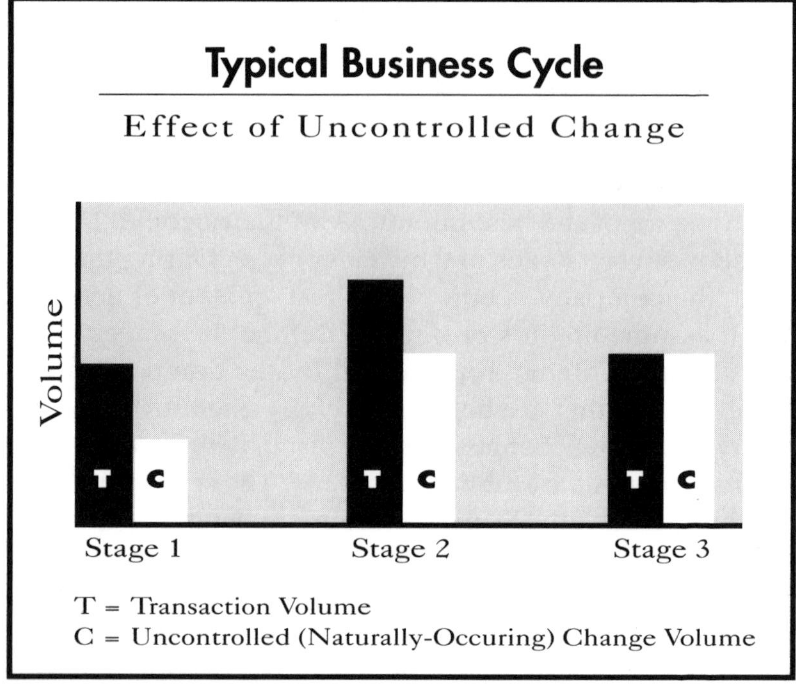

Figure 9.1

work problems on their own. The volume of problems, kept in check by naturally-occurring changes, increases as sales increase. No one notices anything wrong.

The third stage of the business cycle is the downturn. Eventually, all businesses experience a downturn. But naturally-occurring changes only hold the root cause of the underlying problem in check; they don't permanently resolve them. These solutions are usually so frail that any change in the environment will tear them to shreds. So, the number of problems don't fall as fast as sales fall. In fact, the volume of problems may actually grow. As the third stage in Figure 9.1 dramatically indicates, these neglected problems can overwhelm the company, driving the profit down to critical levels. Management rationalizes the company's failure by claiming that the drop in sales was so overwhelming that no one could have stopped the inevitable failure. But they conveniently omit the fact that some players in their market are still in the game. If they do consider this fact, they assign survival to luck when, in fact, the ones who do survive are the ones who used planned, controlled change effectively to solve their systemic problems when they had the luxury of a good market.

10

Chapter 10

We Don't Need No Stinking Policy

With benevolent company leadership and employee empowerment being all the rage, traditional management seems to be on the defensive, always apologizing for exercising its prerogatives and running for cover under the latest business fad. But regardless of all the apologists, managers continue to have a crucial responsibility to their company. It cannot be delegated, ignored, or wished away. Managers are the keepers of the system. They have to ensure that the company's control systems are well-developed, well-fed, and well-understood because everyone relies on the system to answer critical questions of survival and growth.

What we call *the system* is shorthand for the collection of actions and reactions each company goes through when facing a problem. These problems can be as simple as getting the product out the door the afternoon your foreman is out sick or as complex as answering a price cut by a competitor. It can be as visible as the obvious division of labor between the front and back offices or as invisible as the corporate culture. Nonetheless the system exists, and management exists to run it.

Previously we said that the job of the general manager was to design, install and maintain the system. Without someone responsible for making coordinated changes, companies are reduced to jumbled heaps of unrelated and confusing changes. Therefore in order to be a competent manager a person needs to develop six fundamental skills, one of them being knowing how to direct change. Up to this point you've been given a good handle on how change occurs and some of the common tactical tools you might use. We have yet to explain how to decide which changes need management control and which changes should be left to the naturally-occurring domain.

In the 1970s the word *control* took on an almost evil, exploitative connotation. Business gurus invented fads popularizing the notion that systemic chaos was preferable to control. Faced with the increasing chaos of the marketplace and perceived rebellion of the era, management fads embraced the idea that businesses were by nature unmanageable, and therefore the role of management was to emphasize flexibility by removing controls. These pro-chaos fads rationalized their premise using logic that ran something like this: American companies are in trouble. The common *modus operandi* consistent with the evidence strewn about these once-dominate American companies is that they all had massive, top-down control systems. Therefore, these control systems are at the root of American business failure. We're amazed that these appeals had, and continue to have, such a wide following in the face of continued and colossal failures of companies lead by managers following this prescription for profit. Few people following this fad question whether the apparent failure of these discredited control systems was caused by poor application of a sound theory. A similarly constructed argument would condemn Christianity or Islam because people claiming to act according to these religious precepts behave atrociously. Neither argument is logical.

These arguments supporting pro-chaos fads disintegrate when we admit that business systems are man-made systems. They are the antithesis of nature. By intention and design they remove as many of the forces of nature as possible in order to improve our economic well-being.

The history of western business has been and will continue to be a struggle to form order out of chaos and use that order to build wealth. What makes pro-chaos faddism the grave of American business is that so many people have mistaken foolishness as wisdom.

If over-control is not the common source of business failure, what is? The root cause of all business failure in the Middle Ages as well as in the 21st Century is uncontrolled change. All commercial failures can be traced directly to inappropriate uncontrolled change in an entity's systems. It goes like this every time: Management has ample internal and external sources of information disconfirming the current methods of doing business. They refuse to accept this information, and therefore fail to act on it, because they lack the needed fundamental skills. Lacking these skills, they lack the security to move forward. Remember that we said that in order to accept disconfirming information people need psychological safety, the feeling that they can handle all of this bad news because they are confident that they can find a way out. Instead, management hires someone hawking a canned management fad, which only camouflages the problem.

This is not to say that catastrophic economic failures don't occur in spite of well-constructed, dynamic operating systems. Catastrophes can shut businesses down even if management does a superb job of contingency planning. For instance, a fire in our data system may give our competitors a window of opportunity. The Big One in California could immobilize our California brokers. Our investment in Labequam could be nationalized. Planning for these possibilities is prudent management, but no matter how much planning you do you still could be overwhelmed. Just because we know that chaos may dictate the outcome of a future event is no reason to give your life over to the Dark Force. After all, in the end we're all dead, but we nevertheless overcome this ultimate and very personal chaotic event by making plans to improve ourselves in the brief time we're here. Likewise, it makes little sense to turn our productive business lives over to chance just because the cosmos operates on a random-number generator.

Finally, our theory that all business failures can be traced to inappropriate uncontrolled change has to explain activity at the margins—corporate death by natural causes, also known as unforced liquidation. Liquidation is only a failure if it is unplanned, and unplanned liquidation comes about because of inappropriate uncontrolled change of a company's systems. Conversely, planned liquidation or restructuring can be the most logical and fruitful action management can take, given that it is in response to an accumulation of facts. Accepting disconfirming information pointing toward liquidation is a very difficult step for most managers. Nonetheless, even the best run company can find itself on the wrong end of a bad bet that must be covered. Such bet-the-company risks are fully debated and understood *before* they are undertaken by a management team that understands the fundamentals of controlled change. Since liquidation can be a planned response to a risky outcome, such liquidation is not *per se* the mark of failure. Our claim that all business failures result from inappropriate uncontrolled change still holds.

THE RELUCTANCE TO WRITE POLICY

If controlled change is real, it has to occupy physical or mental space and leave a trail. The primary evidence that controlled change exists is the existence of company policy. ***Policy***, whether written or just understood, cradles the proven and essential rules for operating the company successfully over a long period of time. These rules embody the institutional memory and have stood the test of time. Many times they were established or expanded when the company suffered episodic near-catastrophes. Suppose you want to change the way something is done in your company and that the anticipated change violates policy. By definition you're talking about something the company's upper management and institutional memory considers substantial and significant. Otherwise your change would only affect procedures that upper management leaves to you anyway. When your idea is implemented, the company's policy will have to change to accommodate your idea. This change process represents the role of policy-making: To ensure that significant changes are brought to the attention of appropriate people. How policy is changed separates good systems from bad.

Whenever we work with a company looking to increase profitability, the first tool we help develop is an up-to-date policy manual. Typically, upper management pawns the responsibility for writing policy on some unfortunate middle-management person. With such an inauspicious start the project seldom gets anywhere until the middle manager finds a way to re-engage his boss. Why is it so hard to get upper management to do its job in setting policy? And why is policy-setting basic to improving profit?

By now you know the answer to why upper management resists writing policy. Writing a policy manual or updating an old, forgotten one represents significant change. Any change is difficult, especially one that exposes people to great uncertainty and provides little safety. Besides being leery of the consequences of systematic attention to policy-writing, top managers don't want to write policy because they are uncertain where to start, how to write it, why it is needed, and when to stop. Should they finish writing a manual, they have no idea what to do with it anymore than their subordinates. But the fact remains that every company has a multitude of policies on everything from how long to hold accounts payable to how many vacation days can be taken to who gets a key to the office and a parking space. Unfortunately, the only time policy is written down is after a problem arises because it was unwritten.

Another reason general managers are reluctant to write policy is that they feel that if they reduce policy to writing that they will lose flexibility. All managers believe that their business is different, and to a great extent they are right. When asked what makes their business unique, they usually point to intangibles—the maturity of their work force, the "quality" of their product, the superiority of their management. Up to this point they've may have operated with policy manuals covering personnel issues but have had no reason to write one covering operational aspects.

This is the very reason they need to write one. They are ready to take the next step towards improved profitability, and the policy manual is the first step. The policy manual builds the psychological safety necessary to get the management team to move forward.

Last, some top managers resist writing operating policy because they have turned their company over to their lawyers and don't even know it. In the case of writing policy, some attorneys believe they can see into the future. They'll tell you that you should avoid writing policy because it could come back to haunt you in an as-yet unfiled but conjured lawsuit. In a later chapter on decision theory we will show why this kind of "scenario thinking" is bad technique, but for now let's just accept that any advice given by any specialist concerning business practice has to be examined thoroughly by experts in general management, i.e., by people like you. In the case of advice from attorneys concerning policy, use it to help you reduce risk; however, never let an attorney tell you that you should not have a policy manual. If you find yourself getting business advice too often from an attorney, get a new one who spends his time helping you get something done instead of giving you reasons why not to do it.

PLAN, POLICY, AND PROCEDURE

While we might understand management's reluctance to write policy, we won't be able to overcome this resistance unless we build a strong argument of how a well-written, cogent policy makes money. We need to explain why policy is crucial to profit improvement, and why written policy is crucial to sustained improvement. In order to do that we have to build a model of how all businesses operate. While we do that, keep in mind that this model is essential to understanding how change occurs in companies and therefore how policy functions as a change tool.

Before turning to business systems, let's look at an analogous system, a typical family. Families have policies and procedures. Typical policy statements might be "No child goes on an unescorted date before age 15." "Every child will go to college or trade school." "We marry within our faith and race." Few of these policies are written down, but every family member knows that to change them requires a persuasive argument. Suppose that one of the children takes a fancy to someone of a different faith or color and is entertaining marriage or that another decides to quit high school and join a band. The consequences of those decisions go to the root of what the family had accepted as appropriate behavior. Those types of decisions require a complete review of the policy by the "managers" of the family. Father, mother, and maybe the grown children will debate them, and those wanting change will argue vigorously. Maybe the policy will change, maybe it won't. But there is little doubt as to the importance attached to the decision. It will affect what it means to be *this* family. As for the procedures that implement family policy, those might include setting curfews for the children, requiring meeting the children's new friends and their parents before allowing the children to associate with them, and setting aside certain times of the day for study. If one of the children habitually disregards one of these procedures, the reaction of the parents and the family as a whole is less intense than if the child jeopardized basic policy and values. As for an example of written documents backing up procedure, it's not uncommon for some families to keep a board near the back door where everyone posts their whereabouts or weekly chore assignments.

The analogy of policy and procedure in a family fits quite well with business systems. While businesses are not families, they are collections of people who need to know the basic rules of conduct and operation. The first ingredient in any business operating system is the hierarchy of plan, policy, and procedure. Later we will make a distinction between procedures and instructions, but for now we'll lump them both into procedures. All businesses have them, and you'll realize that these distinctions are valuable tools to controlling change. Also for the moment let's put aside the role of documentation in operating a company. Let's assume that we're looking at a pretty typical business that is marginally profitable.

At the highest point of any business operating system is its plan. While the business plan might be written, it is seldom so in many mature companies. Whether written or dwelling in the company's collective subconscious, the ***plan*** contains your assumptions about your market and your place in it. You've got certain basic assumptions about the content of your base technology, your pricing relative to your competitors, the valuable features of your product or service, and your competitive advantage. Your plan sets the boundaries of your business. For example, suppose your primary product is made of plastic. You might define yourself as a specialty plastic molder, a commodity plastic molder, or make no distinction about the process but concentrate on the product instead. You may believe that your competitive advantage is in cost-effective production, in unique product features, or in incredibly fast turn-around. These elemental decisions are the type that reside in your plan.

Your operating *policy*, on the other hand, contains statements about what you are going to do to implement your plan. These *What* statements purposely avoid mentioning who is responsible for executing the policy or how it will be done. Suppose your plan emphasizes your competitive cost advantage. Your policy then would reflect this focus. For example, your company might have the following policy statements:

- Each and every incoming order is reviewed for opportunities to reduce costs. The results of this review are documented.
- Pricing is the responsibility of one department; its decisions are final, documented, and reviewed by management on a quarterly basis.
- Product development will focus exclusively on cost reduction. New product innovation is the providence of our customers, other higher-priced build-to-order competitors, and the marketplace.
- Distributors are relied on 100 percent for selling our product. Distributor contracts are reviewed and approved according to written procedures. The responsibility for distributor relations is assigned to one person (and staff, as appropriate). Distributor performance is reviewed and documented twice a year.

Whether policy is written or not, it still exists. If the policy shown in the above example was unwritten, you still will find evidence of it in the documents the company generates. The order files will have a sign-off from Industrial Engineering about their review of cost reduction, and there might be a fax to the customer asking for a variance in the specified requirements in order to reduce the price 30 percent. Over in Accounting you'll find records showing price/cost reviews. In the president's office you might find all of the distributor files and in them checklists documenting the review and approval of the contracts. You'll also find records of the semi-annual distributor meetings held at a downtown hotel. The fact is that the company has an operating policy that reinforces the business plan.

Procedures, on the other hand, tell you how the policy will be put into place, not what it is. They implement policy. Continuing our example, let's look at how the distributor relations policy might be implemented. The policy says that the contracts are "reviewed and approved according to written procedures." The checklist we found in the president's distributor files is the written procedure that the company follows when they review a distributor contract. *This is an important distinction between policy and procedure* and has a profound impact on how well-behaved your change control system will be. The policy said *what* was going to be accomplished, i.e. that the review would be according to a written procedure, but purposely it does not say *how* that review is to be done. Look at what the policy says about reviewing distributor performance. It says that it will be reviewed and documented twice a year. It leaves the content of the review and the form of the documentation to the procedure. Again this is not a trivial point as you will see later.

THE EFFECT OF DISCONFIRMING INFORMATION ON OPERATING SYSTEMS

In the last chapter we made a distinction between internal and external disconfirming information and controlled and uncontrolled change. Now those distinctions will become clear. Figure 10.1 illustrates the affect of information on the company's plan, policy and procedures. It distinguishes between three sources of information and how much of each type might be necessary before your procedures, policy or plan might change. The horizontal axis plots the relative amount of information being absorbed

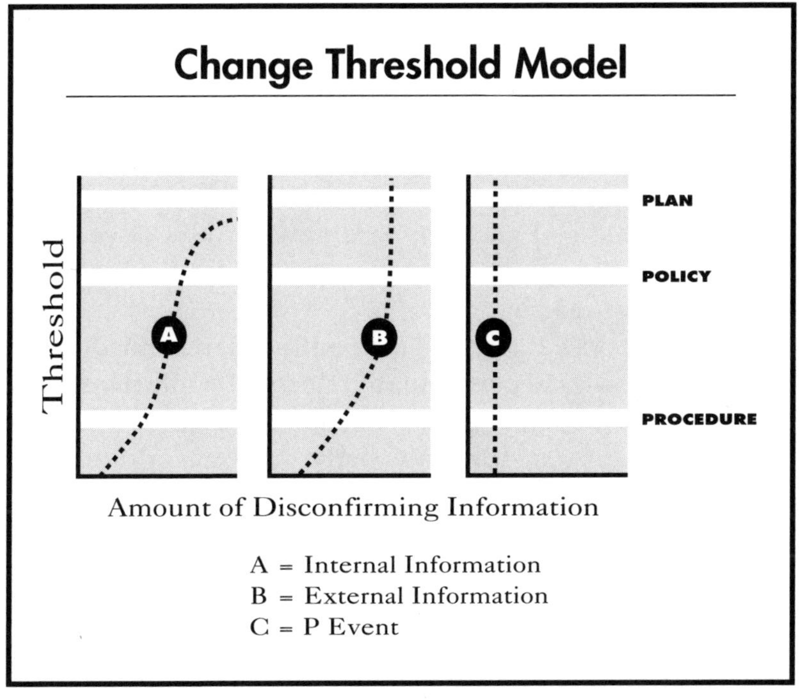

Figure 10.1

by the company. The vertical axis illustrates different thresholds for change. Anytime a line crosses anyone of the three thresholds shown (plan, policy, procedure), that part of the control system will change.

The line labeled "A" shows how internal information might influence the system. It takes a considerable amount of internal information before procedures begin to change, but at some point there is enough readily available that the annoyance of working around a problem brings people together, and a procedure is changed. For our purposes it's immaterial whether this is a planned change or not. (In fact, we have yet to define what a planned change is.) As way of reinforcement, let's again revert to our example. Suppose that the sales department is continually finding skimpy historical information on the incoming order cost review. This is internally generated information indicating that cost review procedure isn't working well, at least according to sales. Up to this point the industrial engineers (IEs) have been solely responsible for this review. The sales department solution to insufficient documentation is to be part of the cost review process. They do what they have to do to be included in the loop. The unwritten procedure is changed and maybe a new form is developed, maybe not. Life goes on, but the procedure for incoming order review has changed.

Now suppose that cost data continues to be inadequate as far as the sales department is concerned while the IEs are concerned that sales' new role in cost review is making the process far too slow and costly. At some critical mass of disconfirming information, a policy change has to be made. This occurs on Figure 10.1 where Line A crosses the policy threshold line. Note that the stated policy said nothing about *who* was responsible for the cost review; it just said each order was subjected to one. As a rule you do not want to include responsibility statements in policy. To be effective, policy statements must be fairly stable while work assignments can and do change, more often than you think. If you make too many responsibility statements in your policy, you'd be constantly issuing new policy revisions, that is if you have a written operating policy.

Now you're gaining some respect for the reasons why we make distinctions between procedures and policy and why writing both of them has such value. Without a written procedure, no one will know whether IEs' sole role as cost reviewer is a convenience of procedure or an artifact of policy. Does general management think that IEs should be the only ones in the loop? If so, that's a policy statement because it's a constraint with the force of policy. Policy is axiomatic thinking that is not easily changed, and when it is changed, general management has to give its consent. If management assigns responsibility at the policy level, the are setting up a semi-permanent gatekeeper.

It usually means that the company has learned, over the years and the hard way, that a particular part of operations demands an unequivocal statement of responsibility. On the other hand, if general management believes that cost review should be a variable function depending on the current best available staff and ideas of the day, then they will keep responsibility assignment out of policy and instead leave it in the procedure domain.

Sometimes information overwhelms policy, and the business plan has to change. This event rarely occurs when internal information is the only driver. Insiders consider internal information as selective, full of built-in bias, and weighted with the hidden agendas of different departments. Even general management is reluctant to change business plans based solely on repetitive and overwhelming internal information. This is why Figure 10.1 shows Line A (internal information effects) topping out before it reaches the plan threshold.

External information works the same way as internal information, but its effect on operational systems is quicker and more dramatic. ***External information*** by definition comes from outside the company even though it may presented internally by an insider. For example, suppose the sales department reinforces its internal information for better cost review with the fact that higher-priced competitors are now beating them on price alone. More functions will be interested in this new external information; no longer is it an intramural issue. The marketplace is offering up disconfirming information. If similar information continues to come in, procedures in many areas will be reviewed to ensure that the company is doing all it can to remain the low-price leader.

At some point procedural changes are just window dressing if what you really need is a policy change. Suppose that the root cause of loosing orders on price is not your cost structure but distributor relations. Suppose that external information says that your big distributors are getting into the production business, and to do so they've cut prices of their own lines to the bone. At this point your policy of relying 100 percent on distributors needs to be reviewed. You may decide you need a policy concerning distributor-manufacturers. Or you may decide that you need a mixed distribution system in geographical areas where distributors are quasi-competitors. Whatever your response, changing procedures will not solve the problem. Your policy has to change.

Another inherent function of written policy is now evident. When you are collating information and looking for the root cause of a problem, you need a way to categorize the seriousness of the problem. In the example above, pricing pressure in the marketplace is an obvious problem for top management. Or is it? It might be obvious to top management that they should be included in the loop, but what if it isn't obvious to the people who actually get the information. Remember Bubba's story in Chapter 9. Because the company was unclear about how information was classified and how changes were made, Bubba couldn't let the "right" people know about his problem because the "right" people were not identified. The right people may not have even known that they were the right people. The power of making a distinction between policy and procedure is that if the root cause of a problem requires a policy change, you *know* you're working with a significant issue.

At some point Line B (external information), unlike Line A (internal information), crosses the plan threshold. Over time we may get irrefutable information that our business plan is suspect. We've changed procedures and we've rearranged our distribution channels, but we still are losing price leadership. Management has got to ask if the basic assumptions about the business are valid. If we change the business plan, then we have to revisit our policies and procedures. This is why categorizing an operating system along the lines of plan, policy and procedure is so robust. The model demands discipline and consistency between levels. While not everyone may be cognizant of these distinctions, they are necessarily affected by them.

The last classification shown in Figure 10.1 is Line C and is called ***P Events***, "P" standing for all the P's in this model: plan, policy and procedure. The source of P-information is almost always external, although accompanying internal disconfirming information may have been building for quite some time. Nonetheless, dramatic and undeniable information tells management that the world has changed and every part of the company's operating system has to change. In the case of a P-event it doesn't take a preponderance of information to force the issue, and the first place management effort needs to be applied is at the plan level. Change of policy and procedures will follow. Some of these recent events include oil prices at $40 a barrel in 1982 and $10 a barrel in 1987, passage of the North American Free Trade Agreement, collapse of the Mexican peso, reunification of Germany, and liberalization of the Chinese economy.

PLANNED AND UNPLANNED CHANGE

So far we've made little distinction between planned and unplanned change. All companies have both explicit artifacts and implicit understanding of this operating model. All change in about the same way because change dynamics introduced in Chapter 6 operate in all companies. But those who plan for change have a plan! That is, they have a systematic way of changing their plans, policies, and procedures. In order to put emphasis where it needs to be, they have procedures for changing procedures. Everyone in these companies knows who is responsible for what work, and everyone knows when he is facing Line A, B, or C changes. These routines ensure that appropriate levels of management are aware of procedural changes without excessive oversight while allowing appropriate personnel to be intimately involved when the situation demands it. They accomplish that by sufficiently and explicitly defining their operating systems such that change opportunities systematically find their way to the right people.

We started this chapter by stating that all business failures could be linked to inappropriate uncontrolled change. It's not that uncontrolled change has to be avoided at all costs. A certain amount has to take place or else you're in danger of over-controlling, i.e., spending inappropriate attention and money on identifying, documenting, and reviewing disconfirming information instead of relying on the efficiency of natural change. So how do you identify inappropriate uncontrolled change? When procedure, policy, or the business plan is changed without management reviewing the underlying disconfirming information. Whenever you cross one of the thresholds in Figure 10.1 and no systematic review of the changed plan, policy or procedure involved takes place, then you've got inappropriate uncontrolled change. *Management's responsibility is defining these three thresholds and building a system that reinforces them.* That is the essence of controlling change in business. Now you know why effective use of policy and procedure is one of the fundamental skills of management we introduced in Chapter 3. Without this fundamental skill you will not be able to use its companion skill of controlling change. The next chapter explains tactically how you can build a system of operating policy and procedure without having to reinvent the wheel.

EPILOGUE

While we've built the case for written policies and procedures, some extremely profitable companies have very little documentation. But these are rare birds. Instead of explicit policy and procedures they have exceptionally consistent and incredibly driven upper-management—usually in the person of an owner or significant shareholder. These people are by definition freaks. Their powers of analysis are superb, and their understanding of policy and procedure is second nature. They intuitively know the difference and marshall their assets accordingly. They are the teachers to the rest of us. But most of us are nowhere near their equals, no more than we can defend against a Hakeem Olajuwon fake or hit a Nolan Ryan fastball. We have to use tools to make up for our shortcomings. To ignore this fact is to reduce the potential for profit and to lose your opportunity to have enduring impact on the companies, divisions, departments and people who look to you for leadership.

11

Chapter 11

Everyone Likes Well-Behaved Children

The previous chapter argued that managers need to appreciate the function of policy and procedure if they are going to have any chance of directing change. Controlled, rational change is the hallmark of sustained profit growth over long periods of time. Every company has an operating system anchored by policy and procedure; how well that system deals with change distinguishes it. While the threshold model illustrates how companies change, it says nothing about how to build and cultivate a healthy system that takes advantage of the model's insights. That is what this chapter does. We'll examine how these systems are built and, in turn, how they become the basic tool for controlling change in your company.

The relationships described in the previous chapter—between policy and procedure and the role management plays in establishing and maintaining them—is a familiar business model that has changed little over the past 100 years. Behind the standards-based management-systems fads of the 1990s is the assumption that the hierarchical model of responsibility and authority is common to all companies. These written standards, created and supported by various industrial and professional organizations, take this model and demand that certain aspects of the company's operations be documented so that they may be audited. Like all fads, this one promotes one element of business over all others, but it had a different twist.

THE PARADOX OF CONTROL AND EMPOWERMENT

Most fads of the 1980s and 1990s stressed, in some form or other, the value and righteousness of flat, presumably non-hierarchical business units. The standards-based management-systems movement, born among the waves of this enlightenment, doesn't fit the trend. The presumption that every business is organized along hierarchical lines (the so-called "command-and-control structure") reflected its heritage. These standards were cousins of earlier military procurement standards. This dubious family tree made some people uneasy and others downright hostile towards standards-based management-systems since the military model of management was dismissed as inappropriate for the private sector. (As of this writing standards-based management-systems continue to grow in spite of this concern. A discussion of their current problems and value is included later in Chapter 15.)

The rush to protect the newly empowered working man and woman by burying command-and-control in favor of *laissez faire* management ignored two facts. First, command-and-control and employee empowerment are not mutually-exclusive. Second, regardless of how flat an organization might be, hierarchial relationships are necessary for work to get done. Just because we refuse to draw a hierarchical organization chart does not mean that the "real" organization has no such tendencies.

For example, in the early 1990s Intel, a leading manufacturer of microprocessors, was featured prominently in the popular business press. Intel was a wildly successful company, and much was made of the role of the company's "culture" in that success. The press was fond of pointing out that Intel's offices were open, allowing free access to anyone at anytime, thereby fostering all sorts of efficient communications and egalitarian feelings between management and the worker bee. We were breathlessly told that even the CEO had his desk in such an open-space environment. This office arrangement supposedly was the paradigm for good business organization. The story matched nicely with the popular management fads of the day. When Intel suffered an embarrassing production problem with a popular processing chip in the mid-1990s, the bloom came off the rose. This same business press revealed that the CEO seldom if ever used his open-space desk (gasp!). He was, according to updated press reports, more a taskmaster closed to other people's ideas than a benevolent leader open to contrarian views.

We tell this story, not as an illustration about Intel, but as an example of how easy it is to mistake form for substance when discussing how work gets done. Whether or not Intel's CEO was what the press says he was or whether or not Intel's success and subsequent problems were related in some way to its "culture" and management style is beside the point. The point is that this type of patterned thinking—Non-hierarchical = Good and Hierarchy = Bad—obscures a basic truth of group behavior and business organizations. Regardless of whether your management style is authoritarian or egalitarian, the people working in your company require some level of command-and-control in order to operate efficiently. Command-and-control does *not* mean that every aspect of the company's operating systems are described in detail. It means that the boundaries between responsibilities and authority are well-established and communicated. For example, it is obvious that the accounting department is not expected to write a law brief on the latest environmental statute, nor is the engineering department going to cut payroll checks. Where those boundaries are set and more importantly how they are changed is the providence of command-and-control and is absolutely necessary in a well-run company of whatever management flavor.

JUST THE FACTS, MA'AM

While command issues can be intellectually separated from operations issues, for our purposes we make no distinction between the two. Our working assumption is that most companies don't distinguish between the two since they rarely discuss either. We've established that the question is not whether you have methods for controlling operations but how well those methods work, especially when under attack. But what distinguishes a good system from a bad one? First and foremost, to be of any use an operating system must be written. Documents are the primary means for understanding, illustrating, and communicating how work is supposed be done. While it may be obvious that writing is a good communication tool, we tend to forget that many times the resulting document is not as valuable as the knowledge gained while composing it. Someone once said, "Writing maketh an exact man," meaning that a writer is forced to develop a solid grasp of his subject while a speaker is allowed to be less precise. Besides forcing us to be more disciplined when explaining ourselves, written operations documents serve as a record of our "best methods" at the time of writing. Many operating documents are only useful when we are trying to understand why something went wrong. Without the benefit of a record of how something was supposed to be done, we have no idea whether our current practice matches our best practice. Furthermore if we believe that something needs to be changed so that we don't make the same mistake, without documentation we really don't know where to start. Everyone will have a different recollection of what the "current state" was or should have been.

QUICK, GET ME A SHOVEL

Just because a system is written doesn't necessarily mean that it is a good one. Documentation is necessary but not sufficient. Such a system could be bad if it either (1) generates excessive, needless, and redundant paperwork or (2) fills up everyone's credenza with thick manuals gathering dust. The first condition (excessive paper) is usually followed by the second condition (dust). These predicaments are not inherent to document systems themselves, but instead reflect their poor construction and implementation by people who have little training building and maintaining them. The assumption that if you can write you can build a good document system is equivalent to believing that if you can speak you can play Othello. If you plan on documenting your management systems (or improving the one you have), you must first address how the documents will be established and maintained. Top management must be involved in more than just signing off on someone else's work. Building or revitalizing a company's document system, whether paper- or electronic-based, is like operating on a vital organ. General management must take an active role in order to understand the ramifications of such major surgery on their company.

There are apparent differences between paper-based and electronic-based document systems, but for the most part how you design a document system is independent of the physical form the actual documents take. Where the issues involving computer-based systems seem to be different, we'll show how they really are essentially the same. For example, a *document system* exists whether or not actual, physical documents exist. The concept of a document is so indispensable that electronic-based information systems continue to refer to their internal records and output as "documents" even if they don't produce a physical piece of paper. A ***document*** is only a tool by which we store information or evidence. It is a record of something in the past. The immutability of ink on paper is a required feature of document systems, and computer-based systems try to emulate it.

SELF-REFERENTIALISM

A document system is a peculiar animal. Many of its documents describe *themselves*, a trait called "self-referentialism". We encounter this feature everyday in other parts of our lives without giving it much thought. Whenever you talk to someone else, you describe bits of the world by using your own personal reference because you unconsciously assume others have had comparable personal experiences. For example, when you refer to "quality" you are referring to an ideal drawn exclusively from your own experience. Self-referentialism—quality, beauty, love, pain, happiness—causes serious misunderstandings, but we seem to muddle through our daily lives in spite of this condition. In fact, the process of maturity is marked by the transition from the child's attempt to unravel paradoxes with the question "Why?" to the adult's acceptance of paradox with the answer "Because."

Self-referentialism explains why it's so easy to chase your tail when you do some quality (there's that word again) thinking about document systems. It also explains why people who work on and around these systems everyday seem a little goofy. You would be, too, if you struggled with paradox every day. Self-referentialism also helps us understand why document systems have an inherent tendency to become unstable, i.e., start generating paperwork by "themselves." It also helps to understand why procedures for writing procedures are essential to maintaining control over procedures. (If that's not self-referential, nothing is.)

In order to understand how to build (or re-build) a document system, we need a way to describe its efficiency, efficiency being a measure of how much the system itself is disrupted when a change in the real world has to be recorded. While the following discussion can be applied to any document system (e.g., financial, environmental, or legal) our examples will involve a company's operating system documentation.

The attributes that determine the efficiency of a document system are:

- How many people get a revised document when job content changes
- How many documents are affected when job content changes
- How many people are responsible for maintaining any particular document

If your document system rates *low* in all three attributes (few people receiving revisions, few documents affected by change, and few people responsible for any particular document), then you will have a well-behaved document system. Surprisingly the number of documents in the system has nothing to do with the document system's efficiency.

These attributes apply to paper-less document systems as well. In fact, these efficiency measurements may be even more important in paper-less systems. It's easy to suppose that computer-based document systems are much easier to maintain since their records are readily changed and have virtually unlimited capacity. But as most people who work with large databases will tell you, what keeps them up at night is not changes that obliterate information but breakdowns in the disembodied information model that describes the relationships between the data in the machine and the real world. Such relational models cannot keep up with unstructured, mindless change. Just because computer-based document systems can keep up with document changes more efficiently than paper-based systems does not mean that they can keep up with turmoil in the real world better than paper-based systems. This points to a central difficulty that computer-based document system designers have that paper-based system designers don't. They have to make managers and users understand that while the system can make information available to anyone and everyone, it's not necessarily in the best interest of a well-behaved, sustainable system to do so for reasons which will become evident.

BE SURE TO SEND A COPY TO MY AUNT IN PEORIA

How can you limit the number of people who must get copies of revised documents? While it seems obvious that you need to control the number of people on the distribution list, how to do that may not be so obvious. First, you have to refrain from distributing paper for the purposes of "keeping people informed." Just because we can copy or E-mail the world doesn't mean that we should. We have seen simple clerical work instructions distributed to more than a dozen people. Most of the people on the distribution list weren't really interested in keeping such close surveillance on the work processes of a single person. On the other hand, should one of those dozen want the information, a well-behaved document system should help them find the information when they feel the urge. If you have a document policy restricting distribution to people actually mentioned in the document itself, you will combat some people's urge to send copies of trivial procedural documents to the entire company.

Even if you restrict distribution to the people mentioned in the document in hand, your system may still be a paper-generator because of an obscure, structural problem: documents with too wide a scope. The more people included in the body of a document, the wider the required distribution. The more activities discussed, the greater the likelihood of duplicate and conflicting information. For example, suppose your clerks in order entry are now required to date stamp each order when it hits their desk. If that change requires distributing the revised instruction to the entire department or worse to people outside the department, you've written a document that has too wide a scope. This usually happens when *instructions* are imbedded in documents that ostensibly describe how *procedures* work. Furthermore if you have a tendency to describe too many activities in one document, the chances that another document also describes the same activity increases. When an operational change occurs affecting this repeatedly-described work, revising the redundant documents is more difficult than it would have been if you severely restrict the scope of each document.

To put the brakes on the natural tendency to expand rather than contract document scope, you need a policy that limits the length of procedures and instructions to five double-spaced pages with 1″ margins and 10-point fonts. You have to be that specific because people will start playing with margins, spacing, and fonts in order to keep within a simple page limit. Should a document begin to grow past the five-page limit (and they always do), it should be broken into two, more focused documents.

Counter-intuitively, getting a good score on the "number-of-people-getting-a-revision" attribute usually calls for more, not fewer documents. This means that your document control system is essential to ensuring the system doesn't spin out of control. We'll discuss how you can do this is after we address the remaining efficiency attributes.

WE'RE SPLITTING JOE'S JOB UP; WE'LL NEED TO REWRITE HIS PROCEDURES

How can you limit the number of revisions required when someone changes jobs or when jobs are re-arranged? An operating system that needs major revisions when confronted with ordinary business changes is suffering either from being too specific when describing hand-offs or from a tendency to write documents around people. (A ***hand-off*** occurs when data or physical items are "handed-off" from one department to another across a pre-defined process boundary.) In the instance of being too specific with hand-offs, suppose your order entry procedure uses job titles when describing how order entry works. This is excellent practice when portraying activities within the function under scrutiny, but if this same document continues to use specific job titles when describing hand-off activities, a future filled with necessary but avoidable revisions is guaranteed. Also the revision process becomes much more difficult. Changes in work on one side of the boundary now have to flow back across and show up in multiple documents on the other side, causing an unbelievably chaotic and tangled mess.

Avoid this systemic weakness by restricting job titles to activities within the function being described and using department or functional names when describing boundary conditions and hand-offs. This documentation discipline has to be outlined in your procedures for writing procedures and be re-enforced by vigilant management. It is dull and sometimes tedious, but nothing works as well as upper management returning a procedure to its owner with a note concerning poor documentation practice.

But being too specific when describing hand-offs isn't the only way that a document system becomes difficult to revise. Even if you are careful to avoid specificity when necessary, you may still generate too many revision requirements if you write documents around people instead of processes. In most companies some individuals hold several distinct jobs concurrently, evidenced by the number of people who say they wear "many hats" or that their title doesn't describe what they actually do. At the high-end we have CEOs who are also chairmen of their boards. At the factory level a production scheduler might also be the quality control manager but hold any number of titles—scheduler, QC manager, expeditor, or vice-president. If these autonomous jobs are lumped together in the documentation into one meaningless job title, the document system will turn inside-out when the company expands and contracts. This continuous expansion and contraction, analogous to breathing, makes you split, combine, or re-arrange jobs constantly. Your document system must be stable during this ordinary life process if you want to be able to take advantage of your environment. You can't hunt for elephants if you're on the operating table all the time.

You avoid turmoil in a document system by building the system with an eye on job descriptions, not on the actual people who hold these jobs at the time. If a person holds a job that really encompasses several distinct functions, split her job into as many stand-alone positions as necessary. You can discover these multiple personalities by using the free-form organization charts introduced in Chapter 8. When the company expands and people are hired to take over some of those responsibilities, the document system will hardly notice. When the company contracts, all the positions will still exist, but several may be filled by the same person.

Another helpful technique when designing or repairing a document system is to ask yourself, "What happens to this procedure if the number of transactions doubles or is cut in half? How do we structure work and its controlling procedures to ensure that we don't have to re-design everything each time the company expands or contracts?" Should the company's sales double or be halved, your goal is for the document system to be essentially unfazed. However, at some point significant document revisions will be necessary. When the anticipated changes are no longer at the procedural level but instead pierce the policy threshold, it's time to overhaul the system as explained in the previous chapter.

WHOSE JOB IS THIS ANYWAY?

The last efficiency attribute examines the average number of people responsible for maintaining any one document. A poor showing on this attribute—more than one person, on average, owning any one document—sometimes reflects confusion between *system* maintenance and *document* maintenance. ***System maintenance*** is an administrative function that ensures documents are distributed in a timely fashion to the appropriate personnel; that the latest revisions are available while obsolete ones are withdrawn; and that everyone is aware of and follows the rules, like adhering to procedures for generating procedures. ***Document maintenance***, on the other hand, is concerned with ensuring that the actual information in the documents themselves is the best, most up-to-date possible. These activities—system administration versus document maintenance—serve entirely different purposes. Like the people who wear more than one hat in the company, these jobs may rest in the same person, but they are two very different, distinct, and independent responsibilities.

The easiest way to hobble a system is to make no distinction between system administration and document content. The quickest way is to habitually assign individual document maintenance to more than one person (that is, giving two or more people the "joint responsibility" for the content of a document). This usually happens when you are reluctant to decide who should be responsible for the outcome of a "joint" activity. Common but deadly joint responsibilities are making sales and accounting responsible for order entry, production and engineering responsible for design control, and sales and production responsible for scheduling.

The way to avoid these fatal problems is to expect one function, like accounting, production or inspection, to be responsible for overall document-system administration but to assign ownership of individual documents to individual job positions. It works like this: The system administrator keeps the master list and master copies of the documents, trains everyone on how the document system works, and periodically audits how well it is operating. Each document, when first written and distributed, is assigned an *owner* responsible for keeping the intellectual content of the new document current. If someone other than the owner has a problem with a document (e.g., not being able to find needed information or believing that a revision is required because of a change in work flow), he goes to the owner of the document, not to the system administrator. The owner is responsible for reviewing the proposed change, checking with related functions at the border of the affected procedures, making the required changes, getting appropriate approvals, and submitting the revision to the system administrator for insertion into the system. By separating *system* maintenance from *content* maintenance, system administration gets the attention it needs without being caught up in technical content. By restricting document ownership to the single person with the most vested interest in the procedure, you make sure content gets the attention it needs to remain up-to-date.

At this point you may be absolutely beside yourself, shouting back at this book, "Whaddya mean I can't have joint owners of procedures? It's inevitable that the most important value-added procedures have to be owned by several people! We're a team here!" If you skip over a couple of pages and read the section "Throwing Work Over the Wall", we'll answer your objection. Just remember to come back. If you would like to learn more about designing a document system and can wait to read about the failure of American management, read on.

THE DOCUMENT PYRAMID

The previous document system rules help you get a good system-efficiency score but omit any reference to a method for keeping track of the documents themselves. That's where a document classification framework comes in. In Chapter 10 we discussed the difference between policy and procedure and explained how this distinction is useful for understanding how change occurs. We mentioned that some procedures were actually work instructions, but that esoteric difference wasn't important at the time. We now return to that additional differentiation.

The document pyramid shown in Figure 11.1 is the universal tool used to organize well-behaved, document systems. Along with other ideas presented in this chapter, it forms the basis of most successful document systems regardless of whether we're talking about financial systems, operating systems, air-traffic control systems, welfare systems, or the legal system. This framework categorizes a document by type, ensuring that its scope remains focused and consistent with its place in the system that maintains it.

The difference between procedures and instructions is as important as the difference between policy and procedure presented in the last chapter. ***Procedures*** tell the reader how policy (as described in the policy manual) is implemented. ***Work instructions***, on the other hand, define how one particular job position (person) works within the confines of a procedure. These are two different documents. Suppose you have a policy ensuring that you understand what the customer wants before you accept an order. Part of that policy says, "We have written procedures for documenting contract review." This is a policy statement; it says what you are going to do, not who does it nor how it is done. Underlying procedures outline who is authorized to accept customer orders, who processes the order, and

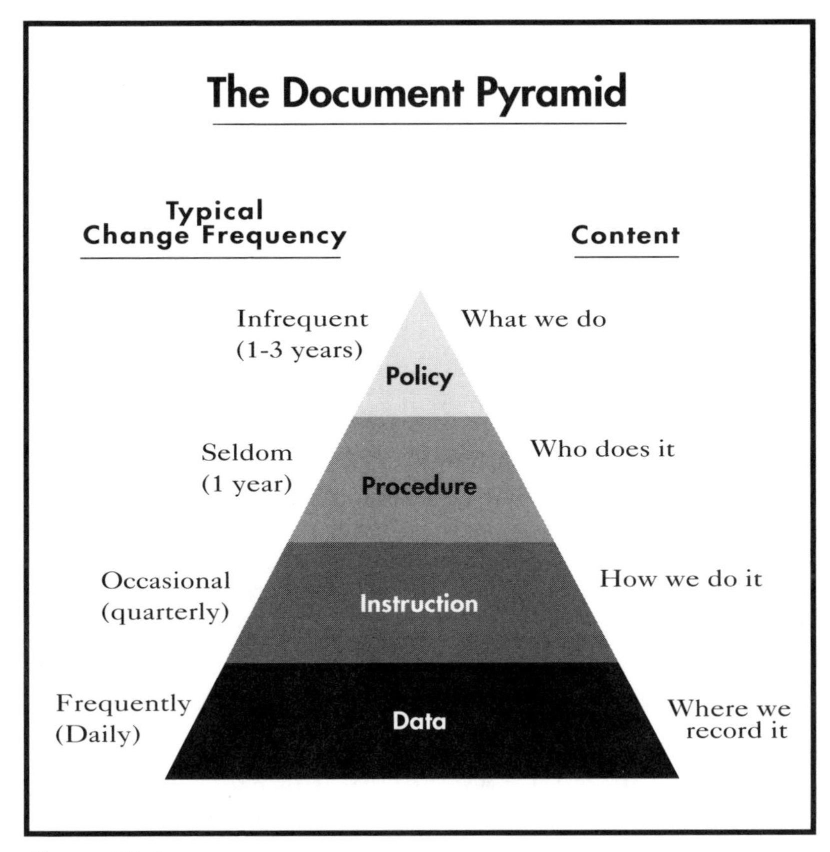

Figure 11.1

which hold-points control the release of the order to production, among other items. On the other hand, work instructions associated with this contract review procedure might include a checklist used by order entry personnel to ensure that all pertinent issues are addressed before they accept a contract. Procedures are boundary descriptors because they define critical boundaries in a process. Procedures control departmental assignments and interfaces, as well as detail the movement of data and material. Work instructions, on the other hand, address how a particular piece of a job is done. It's easy to grasp the difference between these two documents if you envision a work instruction being read and followed by a single person whereas a procedure being read by everyone in a department.

While the distinction between procedure and instruction seems trivial, it is extremely useful when contemplating system maintenance. As the document pyramid shows, separating procedure from instruction reduces the depth and frequency of revisions. Instructions, because they describe the way people do a particular job, have the highest change frequency of all operations documents. If instructions are embedded in procedures, procedures will take on the revision character of instructions (i.e., they will have high revision rates). For example, if the contract checklist mentioned above is embedded in the contract review procedure, every time the checklist changes, the procedure has to be revised. Naturally the procedure is distributed to more people than the checklist since it has a larger scope. Boundary functions, such as sales, production, and purchasing, would be very interested in who reviews contracts since they need to know where they interface with the review function. They could care less what the contract-review clerk's checklist includes. By embedding instructions in procedures, the distribution list now includes people who are either uninterested in the instruction or uninterested in the surrounding procedure. In either case, you wind up distributing revisions to people who have no interest in the change at hand. Note that it is immaterial whether or not you take advantage of computer-driven document systems that claim to make it "easy" to track of relationships between documents. If you don't have discipline within the documents themselves, no amount of outside, pre-canned discipline will help. You'll still inundate people with needless documents. Even if they know little about document systems, they'll know that yours is out of control.

If you do well on all three attributes *and* have a framework for classifying documents, your document system will be well-behaved. When a new or revised document hits the floor, those who get it will know that it contains vital information. They will read it every time because revisions, although not rare, are nevertheless infrequent and therefore warrant their attention. If you rate poorly on these attributes, people will get frequent document revisions having little or nothing to do with their job. Eventually, they stop reading them, and the document system suffocates under its own weight and dies of neglect.

EXERCISE AND REGULAR CHECKUPS

How do we ensure that our document system and underlying operational procedures stay healthy? All systems need periodic check-ups. People should see a doctor every once in a while, and likewise document systems should be checked. This check is called an audit, and it ensures that the underlying documents reflect actual activity and that the system itself is effective. Audits are done in the name of upper management, usually in the name of the premier manager on location. Most standards-based management-systems require a formal, documented audit program. We have found that this audit program is unnecessary as long as the company relies on the documented system to run its business, meaning that the top manager is intimately involved in the system itself. At some point a company becomes too large for top management to have first-hand knowledge about the system's health. Without audits people begin to hide behind "the system." In those cases an audit program is an invaluable tool for top management. The key is that the audit function must be real, not merely a prop used to sell your company's "program" to your customers.

How then do you to tell if your operating policy includes all the elements it should? If you are just starting to document the way things are done in your company, you should consult any number of good management standards such as ISO 9001 or the FDA's Good Manufacturing Practices (even if you're not in the food and drug business). These standards contain more or less generic operating systems elements that can be used in your business as applicable. These elements can be used to form the core of your first (or re-built) operating policy manual. If the policy has an inherent flaw or omits an important element, your documented operating system will generate and communicate the need for a policy review. As long as you listen for it and as long as you understand the fundamental role policy and procedure play in your company, over time you will revise your policy so that it meets all of your needs. The management audit and its supporting nonconformance reporting systems provide the necessary feedback loop to change policy.

THROWING WORK OVER THE WALL

Some people might be eager to point out that the kinds of document systems we've just described are at the root of the problem of American business. The classical picture of this problem shows each department working on its part of the process, boxing their work up, and throwing it over the wall between departments, not worrying about the consequences once that work has been handed-off. But wait: Document systems are not the culprit in this situation, poor management practice is. Document systems can only describe and implement management policy. Basic to all systems are (1) embodiment of best practice gathered through the lens of experience and (2) feedback. If management neglects to establish feedback tools, like nonconformance reporting, corrective action systems, and periodic multi-discipline system reviews, the document system will not work even when people, caught up in the system, employ their best intentions. Unmonitored document systems indeed lead to departmental provincialism. But that is a failure of general management oversight. Just because management decides to abrogate its responsibility for maintaining system health because they haven't a clue how document systems work is no reason to abandon systems altogether. The transmutation of a documented operating system into ad hoc, self-empowered work groups is evidence of degenerate management, unschooled in the fundamental skills needed to run a business.

Finally, let's revisit an idea we stated as fact at the beginning of this chapter, that command-and-control as reflected in documented operating systems does not preclude employee empowerment and flat organizations. It is easy to get lost in a discussion of how to build or re-build a document system and forget the importance of content and context. A lesson of World War II provides a stark example of the importance of the peaceful coexistence between control and empowerment. When comparing and contrasting the German and Russian soldiers facing each other in the Eastern front in 1944, it has been commented that the German soldier was extremely disciplined and considered by many to be a more skilled combatant to the Russian fighter, man-to-man. However, German training also emphasized individual initiative and responsibility; that is, the common German soldier was, as part of his strict training, empowered in the sense of the word as it is used in today's fad management movements. This paradoxical emphasis on discipline and initiative allowed German units to survive incredibly desperate battlefield situations on the Eastern front.

Such empowerment was not unique to the German fighter nor unique to the times nor unique to the armed forces. The point here is that feebleminded- and patterned-thinking in American business has lead to the wholesale disenfranchisement of an entire fundamental management skill—the comprehension of the role of policy and procedure in running a company. The overriding concern of the purveyors of management fads is to present simple-minded solutions. Seeing through the paradox of the coexistence and co-dependency of control and empowerment is complex. It does not lend itself to formulaic, faddish solutions but nonetheless can and must be approached by successful American general managers and their support staff.

12

Chapter 12

Decisions, Decisions

At this point we've discussed four of the six fundamental skills of general management: profit fixation, technical literacy, change dynamics insight, and the care and feeding of policy and procedure. Common to the practice of all of these fundamental skills is good decision-making. While it is a cliché that good managers make good decisions with a minimal amount of information, few can explain how they think about alternatives and chose one over another. However, a good manager needs both a basic understanding of the common decision-making mistakes and knowledge of a few decision-making aids.

GIMME, GIMME, GIMME

Before diving into a brief study of decision theory, we need to address and then set aside our simple-minded attention to the chronic lack of information (or conversely, our fascination with the brave new world of unlimited information). The core question is: What relationship, if any, is there between the amount of information and good decision-making?

One of the tenets of decision theory is that all decision makers are limited by the cognitive capacity of the human mind; it is a fact that humans are unable to hold more than a handful of related ideas or hypothesis in their minds at any one time. If we try to collect more than our cognitive limit, our minds must drop something off the list in order to pick something else up. What that cognitive limit might be is the subject of extensive clinical testing and hypothesizing and is for our purposes unimportant. What is important is that even if you have an astronomical IQ or a photographic memory, the human mind is severely restricted when it forms hypothesis based on perceived relationships among sets of data.

This basic limitation implies that to make good decisions you must not only be aware of this handicap but also find ways to work around it. Mediocre managers who cry about inadequate data are missing the point. They believe that their superior decision-making skills are hostage to their lack of data. Assuming that more data yields better decisions is the most basic fallacy of decision-making. Once you reach your cognitive limit, more data usually confuses you unless you have a systematic method for overcoming this natural limit.

We all have experienced our own tendencies to over-rate our ability to make better decisions with more data. It usually shows up when you have to make a particularly expensive decision. Let's say you are deciding whether you should buy a new car. You think you are on the brink of making the big decision, but you want just a little bit more information. When you get it, you find that instead of helping you with your decision it moves you either further away or sideways along the decision tree. Your frustration level increases. You may even decide to revert to the tried and true method of your childhood, "Ennie, Meannie, Miney, Moe." The problem you face in these situations is not with the data; it's with your ability to make sense of it.

In order to develop tools to help us improve our decisions, it helps to explore the most common blunders. After all, to find a cure you first have to understand the disease. The errors of judgment we'll look at are only a few of the many that have been identified by researchers, but we think they represent a good discussion of how well-meaning managers make bad decisions. These errors include groupthink, over-estimating control versus chance ("the illusion of control"), framing, sunk costs, representative thinking, availability, and ordering.

POLITICS TO THE RESCUE: THE ORIGINS OF GROUPTHINK

Much research has gone into how people make decisions, both individually and in groups. The discipline is called *decision theory* mainly because we can only theorize how people go about making decisions. In America the discipline gets a regular boost from politicians and military planners because they occasionally make tragic decisions that later find their way into the evening news. More importantly and regardless of the embarrassment factor, national politicians and military leaders are acutely aware that their decisions can save people or condemn them. With this kind of weight on their shoulders they want to be sure that they know how to make the best decisions possible. They also have a long tradition of keeping accurate notes of their discussions and decisions so that history can benefit from their wisdom and avoid their mistakes.

Our first example of decision-making bias comes from Irving Janus who wrote "Victims of Groupthink" in 1972, which was later expanded into his book *Groupthink: Psychological Studies of Policy Decisions and Fiascoes*. In it he uses both successes and failures of momentous political decisions to show how group dynamics can distort rational decision-making. His arguments are particularly persuasive because most of us have seen groupthink at work in our companies, but without Janus's exposé it is not apparent what the disease might be. Janus struggled with the paradox that seemingly bright and motivated political leaders occasionally make exceedingly poor and dysfunctional decisions even when copious amounts of good information are available. While he gave many examples of groupthink, his most memorable were his treatment of two crisis of the Kennedy administration, the Bay of Pigs fiasco and the Cuban missile crisis. In each case the decision-makers were the same and the emergencies occurred within a year or so of each other, but they had radically different outcomes. One is seen by some as the lowest point of Kennedy's short administration, the other as one of its highest.

Janus defines ***groupthink*** as "a deterioration of mental efficiency, reality testing, and moral judgment that results from in-group pressures," but any one-line definition doesn't do justice to groupthink's infectious effects. In its most insidious form, groupthink attaches more importance to group cohesiveness and consensus-building than in ensuring that the chosen action plan is rooted in reality. While Janus looked at national policy-forming groups and geo-political issues, comparable symptoms of groupthink are present in most management groups. The level at which groupthink tendencies are resisted is, to a great extent, a predictor of how well the management group will be able to generate robust alternatives to problems and thereby choose a good solution.

Groupthink manifests itself in several ways. We regularly encounter managements that have an unrealistic belief in their superiority and invincibility, which of course leads to an under-appreciation of the competition. This feeling of invincibility comes from the group's over-estimation of the personal abilities of the individual group members (i.e., everyone is impressed with themselves). This trait in turn affects the company in a variety of ways besides poor decision-making. For example, management tends to dismiss their difficulty reaching consensus when negotiating with unions, customers, vendors and competitors. It's hard to find common ground if you believe the rest of the world is occupied by dolts and inferiors.

Managers exhibiting groupthink tend to rationalize any disconfirming information that doesn't fit their concept of the world and their position in it. Disconfirming information in general is discounted because it might force the group to rethink its basic beliefs. The pressure to conform is so strong that group members are reluctant to share any misgivings they have about the course of events. If they did otherwise, the cohesiveness of the group might be endangered. A tell-tale sign of this pressure to conform is evident when a member brings up an idea that challenges the status quo; the rest of the group will be quick to bring pressure on the member to actively and loudly withdraw it by vigorous use of accepted thinking. Although we haven't seen it in business management groups, it is said that in severe cases of groupthink certain members appoint themselves as keepers of consensus. They see their role as protector of group decisions by ensuring that disconfirming information is kept away.

How does a group of otherwise bright people succumb to groupthink? Usually they have built close bonds by weathering a particularly difficult time together. During this period of group formation, the actors get a tremendous amount of confirming and reinforcing information. Ultimately, the group emerges from the original crisis or challenge with an overwhelming confidence and camaraderie. Such bonds developed during the course of business battle are especially difficult to challenge, much less abandon.

Eventually, groupthink will destroy the management function of a company. An isolated, overly-conceited, and obsessively protective management group is not open to change based on objective evidence. Their decision-making prowess is sterile, and the market will exact its tribute. But meanwhile, the people who depend on these people for guidance are the ones who suffer.

The Bay of Pigs/Cuban Missile couplet is a dramatic example of groupthink because it both illustrates groupthink in action and shows that groupthink can be overcome. The

Bay of Pigs was a 1961 CIA-directed invasion of Cuba by a brigade of 1,400 Cuban exiles with the audacious objective of fomenting an uprising in the countryside. CIA planners predicted that this revolt would ultimately lead to the overthrow of the Castro-led government. The invasion was in the planning stages when Kennedy became president. His team had three months to consider the CIA plan and accept, reject or modify it. As a result of their decision to go ahead with the invasion, 1,200 of the 1,400 men were taken prisoner over the two-day battle. Thirty years later Castro is still leading the Cuban government.

The official explanation of the fiasco almost exclusively concentrated on the quality of the intelligence information Kennedy had at his disposal. In reality, plenty of pre-assault information pointed to the almost guaranteed outcome; however, Kennedy's core advisors failed to pursue questioning that would have uncovered the group's faulty decision-making process and illusions. Kennedy and his advisors were affected by groupthink, but how did it initially take hold? Janus says that was the result of a long and hard-fought election campaign in which "New Frontier" election hype invigorated the incoming President and his close staff. Although some staff members were comparatively young, Kennedy counted many seasoned political sages in his advisory groups. The feeling of invincibility was all around him, and up until that fateful day in 1961, it seemed to be justified. Of course, self-delusion seldom lasts forever. Sooner or later the system returns to the mean.

In failure Kennedy was lucky—lucky in that his first prominent presidential decision was such a total and obvious disaster that his inner circle was shaken to their boots. They were forced to question one of their treasured myths: their invincibility. This P-Event called into question all of their plans, policy and procedures (see Chapter 10). If their first geo-political decision had been successful, it would have reinforced the illusion that their decision processes were healthy when, in fact, they were not. Of course, that decision couldn't have been the Bay of Pigs but some other decision that—with a little luck—could have turned out right. No amount of good luck could have overcome the groupthink planning of the Bay of Pigs.

The Cuban Missile Crisis occurred roughly a year after the Bay of Pigs fiasco. On balance its outcome was favorable for the nation. The same presidential group that bungled the decision on the Bay of Pigs performed admirably during the missile crisis. How did they make the change? While groupthink wasn't part of Kennedy's vocabulary, he knew intuitively that his process for eliciting advice from his advisors had to change. Many of them after the Bay of Pigs said publicly and privately that they had early misgivings about the assault but felt that such thoughts would have been disruptive rather than constructive. Using the tragic lessons of the Bay of Pigs, Kennedy radically changed his group management approach. Early in the missile crisis he made his objectives clear to his advisors, and once made clear, he also made clear that he expected vigorous and open debate. He changed the way he held meetings and tended to give more time to opposing views than confirming ones. He changed the entire decision process.

The full-scale assault on groupthink would not have been possible had Kennedy not lead it himself. As with the other five fundamental management skills, decision-making requires decision makers. A good staff cannot make up for a poor manager. To believe otherwise is wishful thinking.

GROUPTHINK IN THE BUSINESS WORLD

While we're sure you can think back over your career and find examples of groupthink at work, a particular press story comes to our minds. In 1995 L. V. Gerser, the CEO of IBM, reorganized his top management team even though they had a very profitable 1994. He pointed out that while the profits looked good they were so because of good luck, not good execution. He emphasized that while fat profits are nice, they are only sustainable if they result from a plan. Although he didn't use the word "groupthink," he was ensuring that his management team avoided it by seeing the world for what it was, not for what they wanted it to be. The arrogance tag that IBMers have had in the past wasn't put there by customers and competitors out of envy; there had to be substance to it. Past IBM management must have unwittingly allowed groupthink to take over their company and reinforce a company-wide superiority complex of mythical proportions that diminished its ability to accept disconfirming information.

ILLUSION OF CONTROL

The next decision-making deficiency comes in many flavors. Basically, it causes us to overrate the amount of control we have over the outcome of a planned event. Two of the most familiar flavors are what we call *one-sided chance* and *denial of the mean*, which are different sides of the same coin.

At first glance it seems odd that a book that emphasizes the role of planning in successful business would conversely emphasize that people tend to over-emphasize the amount of control they have over their lives or their businesses. But these are not mutually exclusive positions. The fact that in most cases probability is a much better gage of outcome than the skill of the player is something we have to inject forcibly into our planning and decision-making. Otherwise, we develop dysfunctional plans that omit a basic truth of the world we live in.

Assigning our triumphs to our personal strengths and skill but relegating our failures to bad luck or chance is the most common manifestation of illusion of control. Few of us consciously assign our triumphs to luck and our failures to personal weaknesses. In other words, many of us only accept a probabilistic world when we want to rationalize our shortcomings, thus the name ***one-sided chance***. We like to believe that we affect a good outcome more than we actually do.

An example of someone taking advantage of our tendency to engage in one-sided-chance errors is state-run lotteries. When Texas lottery officials first introduced a six-number lottery, they did not offer a feature common and available in other states with more mature lotteries: machine-generated random numbers. Ostensibly this was because the "system and equipment wasn't ready" to issue so-called Quik Pick numbers. On the contrary, it could have been. After all, the contractor running the Texas lottery ran lotteries in states offering the Quik Pick feature. Rather, lottery officials knew that if they offered this feature early in the lottery's introduction, they would diminish the illusion of personal skill and control over picking winning numbers. Television ads for the Texas lottery overwhelmingly emphasized method and skill over chance when addressing success.

In business, assigning good financial outcomes to your skill and poor financial outcomes to bad luck (e.g., a bad market) is delusional. Good or bad financial outcomes are a consequence of both skill and luck. The trick is determining how much of each element might be responsible for a particular outcome. Suppose your good fortune was almost entirely because of a good market, and if you had better skills, you would have made an even bigger profit. If you are inclined to assign your success to your skill, you will avoid making any changes to your approach to business. "If it ain't broken, don't fix it." When the market does turn against you, you will be in much worse shape than had you taken advantage of a good market to improve your operations. Instead, you spent precious time congratulating yourself on the good job you were doing. Conversely, suppose your poor results during good times was entirely because of poor decision-making, but you assign it to bad luck. The outcome is similar to thinking erroneously that good fortune came from great management, but it comes much quicker because you were unable to make money even in good times.

Denial of the mean is similar to one-sided-chance errors. It is very hard to accept that most processes have a mean and that the best predictor of an outcome is the mean. Several examples will help illustrate. Take personnel evaluations. Supervisors historically get frustrated with employees because they seem to be inconsistent. A particularly difficult employee, on occasion, will perform admirably; an exemplar employee will have a bad day. In the case of the difficult employee, just about the time a supervisor believes that the employee's troubles are over, the employee again disappoints. There is little mystery what has happened. The employee's behavior clusters around an average. A good manager will have a systematic way of assessing that average performance level. A poor manager will continue to be bewildered with this "inconsistent" performance, seeing a pattern of improvement or diminishing performance where there is none. The manager essentially refuses to believe that a system (the person's behavior) reverts to its average.

A second example of denial of the mean is typical company financial forecasting. The ability of a company to generate profit is generally stable over short periods, say a year or two, unless it is going through some radical refinancing, restructuring, or similar upheaval. However, many large companies require their divisions to generate monthly rolling 12-month predictions of profit and cash flow. Because of the technology of spreadsheets, these reports are dutifully generated. They usually show upward trends in all of the important criteria even if the historical average is flat. If they show deteriorating conditions, the deterioration in the future months will always be forecasted to be less severe than the historical average. This is a denial of the mean. The best forecast is your current mean performance.

You can also find examples of people denying the existence of the mean in articles written by people who should know better. An article in the membership journal of the American Society for Quality Control explored the different ways winners of the Malcolm Baldrige National Quality Award enhanced intracompany communication. In it, a director of employee communications at Motorola was quoted as saying that he depended on face-to-face meetings between employees and managers to get the word out about company policy and goals. While he admitted that reliance on the supervisors made good communications a function of the skill of these managers, he said this hadn't been a problem with Motorola. Besides smacking of groupthink ("We're different, we're smart, we're invincible."), his statement totally ignores statistical reality. Motorola had over 132,000 employees at the time. There is no way anyone can build a system of supervisory training and performance evaluation that eliminates the bell curve in a company that size. The manager was implying that Motorola had some mysterious way to take a population of, say, 500,000 or more potential employees and filter them so that Motorola could identify and avoid the poorest performers. This is the only way that average supervisor performance at Motorola could exceed that of the average corporation. It did not, and it could not. In such a large worker population you cannot avoid average performance no matter how smart you think you are. Making decisions based on denying the existence of the mean is not rational.

Last, take a typical sport like baseball or the stock market. Invariably in the middle of the baseball season the sports pages will be full of stories that a certain struggling pitcher has turned the corner and is back to his old form. Or the financial pages will say that some nag stock has finally come around and will be the next Microsoft. In either story reality is much less dramatic.

Take the pitcher's situation. On average, big league pitchers develop the same way: Building strength in the minors, getting occasional assignments in the big leagues, joining a major league rotation or bullpen, reaching peak performance level, staying there a few years, and ultimately, deteriorating. That's what the averages say. What they don't say is that on any particular day few pitchers perform at their average. Additionally, few of us are taught that, because of cognitive limitations, perfectly random events—like having a good day or a bad day—*appear* to occur in "lumps" (i.e., people tend to see patterns where mathematical testing shows none exist). This cognitive tendency may be vital to our individual creative and survival skills, but it's an illusion. In sports, they call it a hot streak or a cold streak, depending on our perception of which way the streak is going. However, sports streaks don't exist in the probabilistic, real world, only in our minds. A pitcher who seems to be coming out of his slump is really reverting to his mean performance. One who seems to be diving into a "new" slump is merely exhibiting the fact that on any particular day or during any particular period average performance may be hard to see, but over the longer term it is inevitable.

So if most performances are not average performances, why pay attention to the average? Because it is the *best* predictor of a future outcome. In business if you think you've got a hot hand and bet on it staying hot, on average you'll pull up short. If you compound your decision-making delusion with a belief that your hot hand is a result of skill, then your doubling a bad bet. Your luck may continue, but eventually it runs out. Take choosing a chief executive officer. To some extent board members in search of the next CEO choose the wrong candidate when they say they only look at "results." If they fail to explore how much of the candidate's previous success was the result of a hot hand and how much of it was skill, they may find themselves in the equivalent position of signing a pitcher who starts reverting to his mean performance the day he shows up at spring training.

A NICE FRAME AFFECTS THE PICTURE

The previous decision traps are easy to overcome compared to avoiding ***framing effects***. It has been shown that, depending on how possible outcomes of a decision are worded, your preferences for certain outcomes can be influenced. This effect is most evident when the outcomes of certain alternatives are described as losses or gains. People seem prone to pay more to avoid a loss than gamble on a gain, even when the outcomes are identical. A common story used to illustrate this affect concerns an acquaintance calling you up at 3:00 in the morning. If he says, "Listen, I just figured out how you can make $5,000," you'd likely tell him to call you at a more decent hour. However, if he told you that he found a way to keep you from *losing* $5,000, you probably would stay on the line a little longer. But why should you act differently depending on his proposition? The monetary outcome of either piece of advice is the same, assuming your friend has a sure bet (i.e., this is a riskless decision). In either case you'd be $5,000 richer than you'd be otherwise. In the first case, you'd have $5,000 more tomorrow than you have today. In the second case, you'd have the $5,000 tomorrow that you would have lost otherwise.

This decision error phenomena is exploited by sellers of canned management fads. Take the selling of ISO 9000 quality system registrations in the 1990s. We can predict that most chief executives will respond more favorably to a pitch that such registrations would prevent them from *losing* market share than that such registrations would help them *gain* market share. Let's put you in the position of a typical CEO of the day. Assume for the moment that the chances that this fad can deliver either of its promises—avoiding a loss or securing a gain—are the same and that the size of market you lose or gain will be the same. In such a case, the monetary outcome is equal. In either case if you don't choose to buy into the fad, you'll be poorer for it by the same magnitude. For example, say your division sells $30 million a year. If you do nothing in the first case, let's say your sales could drop to $25 million. You now are $5 million poorer. In the second case if you do nothing, your sales remain at $30 million, but you could have increased them to $35 million. In either case if you do nothing, you'll have $5 million less than you would have otherwise. The presumed outcomes are identical, but the first frame is much more persuasive. As an aside, someone might claim that the second choice, where you increase market share, is twice as good as the first because you would both avoid losing $5 million and increase sales $5 million, thereby netting $10 million. Sorry, the salesperson might try to sell you on that line, but the two claims are mutually exclusive. The only way you could see yourself $10 million richer is if a third outcome is postulated: that registration both avoids losing market share and increases market share. That appeal is used infrequently because it mixes the emotional appeal of loss avoidance with the less fulfilling appeal of obtaining a gain. In any case the predominate advertising appeal of the ISO 9000 fad of the 1990s was fear of losing market share.

Another example taking advantage of framing effects comes from retail sales. A large wine merchant in Texas charges customers for using credit cards. However, this charge is framed as a cash discount, not a credit card surcharge. Why? Because to do so implies a loss, which the customer would want to avoid by not using their credit cards. But shoppers look at the retail, non-discounted price as their frame of reference. If they choose to use cash and take advantage of the "cash discount", that's a gain that they'll be happy with. If they chose to use their credit cards, the merchant ensures that they never come face-to-face with their loss.

These examples show the effects of framing are subtle and difficult to overcome. They are also unrelated to semantics. Researchers have constructed ingenious two-choice tests that, because of framing effects, cause most people to swap their selection when the frame is changed. When told that they swapped their decisions from a positive outcome to a negative outcome solely because the frame changed, and are given a chance to repair their inconsistencies, people more often than not chose to remain inconsistent. The decision techniques we present later may, when taken as a whole, help limit the natural bias most people have to pay more to avoid a loss than capture an equal-sized gain. However, the best long-term solution is to insist that potential outcomes of every proposal you see or develop yourself are framed consistently and preferably as gains.

SUNK COSTS MIGHT AS WELL BE AT THE BOTTOM OF THE OCEAN

A cousin to framing is valuing ***sunk costs***, something most managers learned in finance class but which has application to all decision-making. Valuing sunk costs when making decisions is of particular interest politically in these days of budget constraints. During the debate on continued funding of the Super Collider project, many people pointed out the vast sums of money that had already been spent was justification for continued spending. The question at hand was not whether the monies already spent were spent prudently, the question was whether the additional money that needed to be spent would deliver value in excess of the proposed amounts.

Cost-overruns almost always occur because people honor sunk costs and disregard the lessons sunk costs teach. How else can we explain $350 million public works projects that end up costing billions? Each time additional funds are requested, two arguments are presented. First, "only" an additional couple of hundred million are needed, and second, we've already spent hundreds of millions, which we have to "protect". Two other points are rarely brought up. First, the hundreds of millions already spent over the budget have bought us, at most, the knowledge that we don't know how much this beast is ultimately going to cost. Second, at this point in the project's development we might have enough hard evidence to predict that the benefit of the completed project will never exceed the incremental cost.

Suppose the taxpayer is asked to spend $350 million (on top of the already $800 million spent) on some military weapons system. The contractor admits that changes in military technology and changes in potential threats have reduced the effectiveness of the weapons system to at most $300 million. (This number was calculated by accepting the fact that the weapons system's performance improvements cannot be fully utilized in the new battlefield scenarios, and therefore the supposed improvements are valueless.) The fact that we're being asked to pay $350 million more on a system that will deliver $300 million of value is lost in the argument about "protecting" the original $800 million.

As we said, we honor sunk costs in many other ways. For instance, suppose you were ready to buy a new car. You've decided that your current one is getting up in years and becoming unreliable. You've decided what make and model you want and how much you want to spend. While you are making your decision, your old car has transmission problems, and you shell out $700 to fix it. If you decide to postpone your purchase of your new car in order to get your $700 "back", you are honoring sunk costs. You cannot get your $700 back. The only value your $700 has is confirmation of your decision to buy a new car because indeed your old car is unreliable. If you insist on honoring sunk costs you'll never get a new car because you'll always be trying to get the last dollar you spent out of your old heap.

Another example: Suppose you spent $100 on some expensive tickets to an entertainment event next Saturday. On Friday that certain special someone you've been trying to attract shows some interest in doing something with you on Saturday. You turn him or her down in favor of your original plans, even though you'd rather go for entertainment of a different kind. You are honoring sunk costs. The money has already been spent, and nothing you do will get it back. You're better off looking at that $100 as the price of doing something you want to do (being with that someone special) rather than the price of doing something you'd rather not (going to the event).

Sunk costs can also come in the back door. We know of a *Fortune 500* company that held a sizeable receivable from a management consulting firm. Receivables are sunk costs if you can't recover them. Instead of recovering cash or writing it off, the company agreed to hire the consulting firm for a morale-improvement program in order to "recover" the sunk costs. Of course, the company never viewed the receivable as sunk. Instead, they spent additional time and money making their staff participate in an ill-conceived and generally unwanted program, all because the company's management honored a sunk cost.

Honoring sunk costs in business is different than honoring sunk costs in your personal life, and that may be where the rub comes from. In business sunk costs are not honored because the underlying assumption is that the business is on-going and has an infinite life. People do not have infinite lives and are very aware that they all face the same end-game. If you're 60 years old, you're less likely to start a new career than if you're 35. A 60-year-old must honor sunk costs. He's spent a lifetime building a skill and a career. Disregarding the effort he has put into his life because it is a sunk cost is irrelevant and irreverent. Personal decisions have to recognize that life is finite; economic business decisions don't.

It bears repeating that the only thing that can be brought forward into the future when contemplating sunk costs is not how much you've spent on something so far, but *what you learned* from the money you've spent. While knowledge is transportable into the future, sunk costs are not.

SO, HOW DO YOU THINK HE'LL REACT?

A good salesman we know, when asked how he thinks a particular customer will react to a blind proposal, always reminds us that he has no idea. By doing so he is studiously avoiding representative thinking. ***Representative thinking*** is a cousin of denial of the mean. When you deny the mean, you see trends where none exist. You believe that you can forecast subsequent events of stable systems by relying on short-term, near-time events rather than mean performance. When you use representative thinking, you over-emphasize the importance of one piece of information you possess over others you don't.

In the example of our salesman, he refuses to assign any importance to clues he may have concerning the willingness of his potential customer to buy. Why? Because he knows that he hardly has all the appropriate information to make such a judgment. He might judge that there is a 5 percent chance that his mark will respond to his proposal, based on his hit rate for potential customers in this class. By doing so he is honoring the mean. But to believe that he has a better or worse chance with a particular customer because of other factors is an illusion. For example, suppose he notices that his potential buyer has a big title and works for a big corporation. If he is not careful, he can slip into representative thinking and conjure up all sorts of reasons his hit rate might be lower. He thinks, "Big Titles working for Big Companies have assistants. Assistants can be over-protective of access to their bosses. Therefore, the chances that the blind proposal will get by the assistant is less than average." He just invented a scenario that has less probability of being true than if he were to guess that his target was no longer with the company and therefore never receives the proposal. The fact that we can imagine many possible scenarios of how an event might play out has no effect on the fact that the real world generates more possibilities than we can hope to conjure. Sure, the target has a higher chance of having an assistant working for a bigger company than if he worked for a smaller company and had a lower-level sounding title. But what of it? That may *increase* the probability that our salesman might score a hit based on other scenarios he hasn't thought of. The assistant may be looking for some way to impress the boss and decides to respond to the proposal. The world is too complicated to allow our feeble minds to assess outcomes based on the number of scenarios it can generate. You can almost guarantee that your concept of how an individual will react or how a situation will turn out will be wrong unless, of course, you have access to objective statistics. Then, you'll be wrong only half the time.

A more thought-provoking and personal example of representative thinking is the typical reaction many have when we see an ill-kept person on the street corner and immediately think he is a potential criminal. While it is true that a majority of petty criminals don't dress particularly well, the vast majority of poorly dressed people are not criminals and therefore do *not* warrant your distrust. If you are having trouble understanding this point, see if this makes any sense: Serial killers are for the most part normal-looking. Both Ken Bianchi, the California Hillside Strangler, and Ted Bundy, the University of Florida Co-ed Killer, were well-dressed, articulate serial killers. Does that mean that women should avoid well-dressed, articulate young men? We don't think so.

I SAW IT ON TELEVISION

Availability is perhaps the most frustrating decision-making error because it is the easiest to avoid. It seems the more we know about a certain situation, the more we over-estimate the probability of it happening. Decision theorists say these events are available to us through some personal experience.

For example, if you ask a customer to estimate the percentage defects in your product, he would over-estimate the rate. Why? Because in the absence of hard data he would remember (or have available in his mind) the problems he's had with your product more accurately than he would be able to recall how much product he buys from you.

Availability is also at work at a much larger and more expensive scale. After the *Exxon Valdez* spill in Alaska additional safeguards were mandated in the U.S. tanker fleet including double-hulled tankers. The fact that *Valdez*–type accidents represent only a small fraction of the overall risks of oil-tanker operations and that money might be more wisely spent on reducing more significant and predominate risks was lost in the passion of the moment. The Valdez accident was available: The fact that it happened distorted the more important discussion about overall tanker safety.

Continuing with the oil industry, look at something called "wellbore design." Wellbore design is the arrangement of below-ground equipment used to produce a well. For the most part this equipment is non-proprietary, off-the-shelf stuff, but it's not uncommon for well costs to vary as much as 50 percent depending on who designs and drills the well. Some of this reflects rational differences in risk assessments, but most of it is the consequence of the distortion of availability in decision-making. Wellbore design policy of different oil companies tends to reflect not the long-term experience of the industry but the near-term experience of the individual oil company. If a company has had a recent rash of high-profile blow-outs, it will change its policy toward design and operations in response to the recently available experience. If it has a rash of collapsed pipe, it will beef up associated designs. Wellbore design varies across the industry because base failure rates are ignored in favor of incremental failure rates that are overly affected by episodic, high-profile, available events.

SO, WHADDYA WANT TO EAT?

When you go out to eat, how do you decide what you want? You scan the menu and the first or second item that strikes your fancy, you order. If you could observe yourself, you'd find that more often than not you chose the last dish that struck your fancy, not the first. Later you look over at another table and notice that someone is eating your favorite dish and you missed it on the menu. You just became a victim of ordering.

Ordering in decision theory refers to the tendency we have to choose the first alternative that appears to satisfy our needs. If we continue our search we do so by comparing the subsequent items to the last one which appealed to us. If we find another appealing one, it replaces our definition of acceptable. We continue the search against the last appealing alternative. People in real estate know this tendency well, which is why they usually start out showing you houses you utterly detest and save the best for last.

Ordering indicates two things. First, we stop our search short of exhausting the list. Second, if we continue a search we resort to anchoring our decision with the last acceptable choice. To some extent we have to accept ordering as a natural limit of our resources. At some point we have to say that we are finished generating alternatives and have to make a choice. Additionally, any search for a good answer has to include some scheme for ranking alternatives.

The problem with ordering is that there are better ways to make decisions, though not necessarily when it comes to choosing a meal at a restaurant. While the restaurant example is a nice introduction, it is a weak analogy for business decisions. Few business problems come with a ready-made menu of choices. In business and to some extent in your personal life, if you fail to separate the generation of alternatives from selection, you will suffer from poorer decisions than if you did otherwise. The dysfunctional approach of combining the search with the decision means that you are held hostage by the order that the alternatives are presented. That gives an inordinate amount of weight to your first acceptable (though not necessarily best) alternative. Ideas generated later in your search will be more robust and fulfilling, but poor decision techniques eliminate them before you can generate them.

EPILOGUE

This brief discussion of the decision process was just that, a discussion. We avoided rigorous definitions and thorough theoretical discussions in favor of a leisurely walk through the discipline of rational decision-making. It was a good set-up for the next chapter, which introduces a handful of decision tools meant to help avoid typical decision errors. Decision theory as a discipline is of course much more elaborate than it appears here. If you want to really delve into this meaty subject in more detail, the appendix contains a list of books exploring this subject. We highly recommend a trip to the library or bookstore.

13

Chapter 13

Decision-Making Tools

Identifying the root of a problem is not the same as solving it. In the last chapter we visited the more common decision errors. Some suggest their own solutions while others seem unavoidable. In this chapter we're going to introduce a few tools you can use to improve the quality of your decisions. You won't necessarily use all of them at any one time. Some of them, like decision trees, you may never come back to.

The central idea in all of these tools is that to improve decisions you have to find ways of avoiding the bad ones that lead to disaster. Some people will see this as planning for failure, which they will say ensures failure. We don't deny that success depends, to a certain extent, on psychological factors. Success may indeed hinge on going into uncertain situations with every intention and belief that you will succeed, but turning that thought into a cliché doesn't increase its authority. Planning for failure is the best way to remove the downside, which allows people to be more secure, not less, in their assessment of success. Certain warrior tribes went into battle only after they made arrangements for their funerals. They had no intention of dying. Ensuring that the downside was protected meant that they were more confident of the upside.

PAPER AND PENCIL VERSUS SPECULATION

In Chapter 8 we discussed business meetings and why most are universally dismissed as colossal wastes of time. We touched on the importance of keeping a record of all meetings if we are going to have a chance of increasing their value. More generally you won't be able to improve your business decisions at all if you don't figure out how to use paper and pencil in all decision situations.

It's easy to trivialize the importance of a simple piece of paper and pencil, but bear with us for a moment. Take out the notes from your last meeting. Go through them briefly and circle one or two important points. You don't have to spend more than a minute on this exercise. Once you've marked what you think was important, find someone else who was in that meeting. Ask him to review his notes and tell you what the salient issues were. More than likely you'll find that either he doesn't have any notes, can't find them, can't make any sense of them, or has an entirely different impression about what was discussed and decided. The last problem—disagreeing on what was discussed and decided—isn't really a problem. At least both of you can recall your impressions from contemporaneous notes. The unsolvable problem is that in the absence of meeting notes, any value the meeting might have had at the time is completely lost. You might as well have gone to lunch than had the meeting.

The written word provides the sustenance of civilization. The next time you see a TV news clip of a working meeting of the U.S. President or a congressional committee, notice the nondescript staff people in the background whispering to each other while earnestly clutching sheaves of paper. The next time you channel surf, stop at C-SPAN coverage of someone giving testimony; notice that the witness refers to notes of a conversation she had two years ago. The next time you follow the progress of a lawsuit, notice how testimony based on contemporaneous notes carries more weight than someone's unassisted recollection.

On the other hand, have you ever gone to a business meeting to discuss an important question and no one took any notes, much less issued minutes after the meeting? How often in those circumstances did the meeting degenerate into a forum for unstructured speculation and one-upmanship? Ever been frustrated that after such a meeting all the principles had different ideas on what was decided? Have you ever wished that you could go back and recollect the events of that meeting but know that you never will be able to? This typical portrayal illustrates an irritating trend of today's managers: Many ignore the tools of their trade and feel uncomfortable displaying them, all to the detriment of their work.

A manager who doesn't know how to use a piece of paper and pencil is like a construction carpenter not knowing how to swing a hammer. Neither can do his job. This dysfunctional behavior is surprisingly widespread and seems to be driven by an influential pop culture stereotype that colors management's view of the world. The image of the American power-manager includes: tailored suits for her; starched, monogrammed shirts for him; and for both, a very thin, leather portfolio holding a few clean sheets of paper with an expensive pen for signing those important documents. The updated image has them using a computer, so weightless and small that it fits into that ever-present thin, leather portfolio. Never mind that the streets of Manhattan, Los Angeles, Chicago, Houston and a thousand other business centers are actually populated by men and women in rumpled clothes, lugging 5.5-pound laptop computers in over-the-shoulder bags, loaded with candy bars, computer disks, operating manuals and three sets of keys. They dream for the day they can off-load their white-collar flotsam and jetsam and join the power managers. Disregard the occasional glimpses of the captains of American business at work. They are almost universally overweight, bleary eyed, not particularly well-dressed. They also lug around huge amounts of paper wherever they go.

Mind you, you should rely on your staff to do staff work. Likewise, there's nothing wrong with wearing nice threads. However, the power look—the right clothes and the right portfolio—is a high-maintenance masquerade that can be pulled off successfully by very few people. Most of us will never work a job where we have a staff fully dedicated to supporting our individual, personal effort, even if we reach our goal of running a company, division, or department. If we have a staff, they will most likely have their own work to do in addition to assignments related to our work. We find ourselves in a position that demands we dress the part of power manager but actually accept a different one. We might walk the street looking good, but back at the office, at home, and in the car, stacks and stacks of paper await our attention.

MIGHTY FINE DOODLES YOU'VE GOT THERE

Return to that business meeting where the discussion degenerated into a marathon contest of speculation. Let's put a pad of paper and pencil in front of every participant. At least now they have a prop, and if they get bored, they can draw caricatures of other people in the room. If you are in the room, what will you do with your paper and pencil? First, when the meeting is finished you hope to have some sort of record of the ideas that struck your fancy and maybe a note or two to yourself concerning what you're next action will be. Second, during the meeting you'll be using that paper and pencil to march yourself through some of the decision tools we'll discuss later. Ideally these decision tools are displayed on a flip chart for everyone to see. If your peers aren't up to your speed yet, you won't be using that flip chart, but that's a different problem. You'll still need your paper and pencil to apply these tools for your own benefit.

If you aren't used to making meeting notes, you'll wonder what you should write down. This is the fun, artistic part of your job. Like art, there are a few useful rules, but you still get to react to what you hear and see, and you get to create your own landscape. Rule #1 is that your notes be honest and clear to you. There are no rules on how to organize, what format to use, and what those notes should look like. You will develop your own style. We like to jot down revealing phrases or comments preceded by the name of the actor. If we have a personal reaction or thought concerning the point just expressed, that response shows up in brackets. This helps us get closure on ideas that boiled up earlier but were inappropriate to mention at the time.

In essence, personal notes are a history meant for your eyes. They are your means of communicating to yourself over space and time. The value of a personal record becomes evident when you go back to them weeks later. As you read your notes, you'll notice that they include important items that you could have never recollected without help of a contemporaneous record. For example, you might come across a note concerning Sam's awareness of a particular problem. At the time you scribbled it down, it didn't mean much, but when you read it later, you may be able to put it in some useful context. "I wasn't sure Sam knew about the sales situation back then, but there it is in my notes. Yesterday he told me he didn't know about it until after the meeting." Sam wasn't lying yesterday; he actually believes he wasn't privy to the sales problem at the time of the meeting. His honest recollection differs from the facts. Without notes, his mind is incapable of keeping temporal track of critical events, and in absence of a written chronology it is more liable to invent history than to recall it completely.

Habitual note-takers know how unreliable memory is and that notes don't need to be exhaustive to have value. In fact, personal notes are a work of art, not a labor of engineering. If you get wrapped up in note-taking, believing it to be a structured and demanding process, you'll miss sharp turns in the discussion and shifts in tone and attitude. A short record using key phrases and comments will enable you to recollect much more of the meeting. These notes serve to jolt your memory later, not replace it entirely. Sometimes meetings are so intense that you will be unable to make any notes during them. If that is the case, take a few minutes afterward to reduce your recollections to paper. Better then than later. Better later than never. Our experience is that notes taken within 30 minutes or so of an event, although different from those taken contemporaneously, are a good recollection of business events. On the other hand, you might as well skip it if you can't get it done before the end of the day.

We can say without hyperbole that the invention of paper and pencil was as necessary to civilization as the taming of fire and domestication of wild grasses. You are fortunate, through education and opportunity, to be able to apply its power every day. It allows you to overcome your natural cognitive limitations, it multiplies your intellect, and it serves as the essence of leverage in your work. It will allow you to order alternatives and thereby is the basic instrument of good decision-making. Don't abandon it just because popular culture says that people with paper and pencils are nerdy pencil-necks. The most successful, richest, self-made people in America are nerdy pencil-necks. There's got to be a connection.

SO MANY CHOICES, SO LITTLE TIME

You may still question our homage to pencil and paper. But as we lay out the fundamental elements of good decision-making, it'll become very evident that good decisions cannot be made intuitively. Now that we've put a pencil in your hand and a piece of paper in front of you, let's talk alternatives.

The first step in good decision-making is defining alternatives. Every problem needing action is a dilemma—a decision that requires choosing from alternatives that on the surface seem equivalent yet may not be. The first alternative in any list of alternatives is the status quo. The question, "Why change?" is cardinal in the change framework presented earlier in this book because it forces decision-makers to recognize that the status quo must be fully repudiated if we are to move on to other alternatives.

The next routine and predictable mistake decision-makers make, after ignoring the cardinal question, is concocting a flimsy list of alternatives. This is the first place a piece of paper and pencil comes in handy. Since your cognitive limit is five (plus or minus two), you can't keep all of your alternatives in front of you, so to speak, unless they are physically in front of you. So whip out a piece of paper and start listing as many alternative solutions as you can. Don't think about how good or bad a particular alternative is; just jot them down. There will be plenty of time to figure out their attributes and assign them a rating.

Suppose you're unhappy with your present job and are trying to look at your alternatives. If you limit your list of alternatives to either staying with your present company or finding another job, it's too easy to decide to look for another job. You've just limited the quality of your decision. Your alternatives were limited by your hasty move to the next problem statement, "What other jobs are available?" You need to stay at the "Why change?" question much, much longer. Why are you unhappy with your present job? Depending on the answer to that question, you might come up with this list of alternatives:

- Do nothing: Stay with my current job
- Drop out and go on the road with a bar band
- Ask for a transfer to a different department
- Go back to school
- Change professions
- Move to another part of the country
- Take up an avocation
- Seek counseling
- Ask your spouse to go back to work
- Ask for a raise
- Get a pet
- Have an affair

The more alternatives you can generate without prejudice, the better chance you have for clearly defining the problem and finding a good solution.

THE 1,000-POUND CANARY SITS WHEREVER HE WANTS

By writing down your list of alternatives, you've avoided putting a halo on any one alternative and prevented, as best you could, anchoring yourself to an alternative generated early in the process. We can't overemphasize the importance of generating alternatives without concern about how realistic, practical, or sane they might be. Ignoring the attributes of an alternative lets you include some outlandish possibilities that, while initially outrageous, may lead you to think of related but more practical possibilities.

Many decisions don't have to go much further than listing alternatives because one choice becomes the obvious *dominate alternative*. In our example, if this were a real list of apparently equally attractive alternatives, the dominate one might be to seek professional counseling.

On the other hand, even if you don't spot a dominate alternative, you might be able to narrow the possibilities down to a few. Suppose you narrow it down to two choices: "staying with your current job" or "asking for a departmental transfer." Rather than getting over-exercised about the decision, write the competing alternatives across the top of a sheet of paper. Then write the pro's and con's beneath each. In our example your list might look something like this:

STAY	ASK FOR TRANSFER
Enjoy my co-workers	New friends
Can't stand my boss	New boss
Good money	Less money
Have a track record	Low seniority
Topped out	New potential for growth

A simple list like this makes it clear not only what you consider important about your decision, but what risks are inherent in your decision. Also it is one way to look availability right in the eye. You may remember from the previous chapter that availability is the decision error that makes us believe outcomes available to our memories are much more likely to occur than they really are. For instance, most people believe that it is more likely that they will be murdered than is the case because they hear about the "high crime rate" on the evening news. Lists like the one above always make the unknown, future state look riskier than something familiar, even though the amount of risk may be equal. For instance, you might like your co-workers and therefore believe that staying in your old job will ensure a continuing relationship, but you don't consider the probability that they themselves might quit. You can't stand your boss and figure that the current situation will last forever, but you underestimate the chances that she may transfer before you.

Listing the pro's and con's of a couple of major alternatives helps you focus on which attributes are more important than others. Suppose you start the process thinking the "potential for growth" attribute overwhelms all the others. After listing the other attributes you may find a balance between attributes that wasn't possible to see if all you did was think about the problem instead of writing it down. If after looking at the list you still can't decide, you can either flip a coin or get more rigorous, as we will show.

WE'RE RUNNING A SPECIAL ON OUR MINI-MAX SOLUTION TODAY

But before we get more rigorous, we need to touch on a line of thinking called the ***mini-max solution***, that is, minimizing your maximum regret. Using the previous example, suppose you decide that you're going to ask for a transfer. Before you act on your decision, ask yourself, "What's the worst that can happen if I go ahead versus what's the worst that can happen if I stay? Which decision has the potential for encompassing my biggest regret? Is there anyway to minimize my maximum regret?" Suppose you would regret it more to ask for the transfer and not get it than you would just to stay in your old job. Why might that be? You could be concerned that your friendly co-workers might treat you differently back at your old job once the cat was out of the bag. Since your relationship with them is very important, you may not want to jeopardize it. You could also be concerned how your already poor relations with your boss might be affected by an unsuccessful transfer request. While you may still move toward that transfer, mini-max thinking indicates that you should take time to gather more information about the probabilities of getting that transfer. You might also do more planning for your re-entry into your old job if the odds go against you. The mini-max solution allows you one last chance to check the validity of your decision. It asks the decision-maker to develop a worst-case scenario and see if it can be sustained without taking a fatal hit.

Managers give the mini-max solution too little attention. They tend to believe that alternatives have only one possible outcome. Unfortunately those predicted outcomes are generally weighted toward the manager's preconceived ideas about the desirability of the alternative. For example, new product introduction plans are notorious for over-estimating the good things that can happen while ignoring the downside. A pre-launch mini-max review will at least show where the company is most vulnerable, and while not necessarily killing a proposed action, it might be able to reduce the impact of a poor outcome.

TOO MANY CHOICES AND SO LITTLE TIME

If you can't narrow your alternatives down to one or two and make a choice by simple inspection, you need to use more sophisticated decision-making tools. If you're struggling with a real dilemma, a cursory review of the list of alternatives may show several are equally attractive for different reasons. One will seem particularly good for one reason while another could be the hands down favorite for an entirely different reason. You need a quantitative method to help rate each alternative against its competing alternatives. The alternative whose assumed outcome has the best rating is your choice.

Let's try a new example. Say that you have decided to open a distribution facility in New Jersey. To make the example simple, suppose you've narrowed the choices to two alternatives. Location "A" is in a heavy industrial area near a major interstate interchange. Location "B" is in a light industrial area in a New Jersey suburb. You list the decision attributes.

- Location relative to truck transportation routes
- Location relative to trained work force
- Lease cost
- Length of lease
- Proximity to local vendors
- Physical condition
- Alternative lease opportunities in area.

This list of attributes is no more sophisticated than one generated for the example of choosing whether or not to ask for a departmental transfer, except that it's stated without any reference to the alternative we're rating. Your next step is to compare each of the two alternatives and give them a rating in each of these areas. The rating you give is arbitrary, so let's choose 1 (bad) to 5 (excellent).

Location to truck transportation routes: The best location would be near a major interchange, because that will keep your turn-around time down. The worst would be in a rural area served by a two-lane black-top 30 miles from the nearest interstate. With this in mind, you give Location "A" a rating of 5. Location "B" isn't like being 20 miles outside of Wink, Texas, so it doesn't deserve a 1, but you give it a rating of 2.

Location relative to trained work force: The best location would offer college graduates at prison inmate wages. The worst would give you prison inmates at college graduate prices. You give Location "A" a 2; Location "B" a 4.

Lease cost: This is easy one. The best location would give you rural West Virginia rents in New Jersey. The worst would give you Tokyo rents in New Jersey. In this case Location "A" and "B" are about equal, so you give them both a rating of 3.

Length of lease: This is an interesting one in your case. You want a short-term lease because you're thinking about minimizing your maximum regret in this attribute. Since this is a new location, it may not work out, so you want to be able to pull up stakes easily. The best alternative would give you a month-to-month lease; the worse would lock you in for a couple of years. You will not entertain anything longer than two years. Location "A" wants a one-year lease, which is not bad for prime industrial lease property in New Jersey, but no prize. You give it a rating of 2. Location "B" will give you month-to-month after six months. You give it a rating of 4.

You get the picture. Decide how the best and worst alternatives would rate for the attribute, even if such choices don't exist in the real world. Then, rate each alternative against this yardstick. Give each alternative the same rating if they are essentially the same. You should, however, still give them a rating consistent with your best/worst case. Later, we'll show you how to rank alternatives and weight your scores, so keeping true to your rating system is essential.

At this point you've got a piece of paper with the following information.

	LOCATION A	LOCATION B	LOCATION C
Attribute			
• Transportation	5	2	5
• Work force	2	4	5
• Lease cost	3	3	5
• Lease length	2	4	5
• Proximity to vendors	5	2	5
• Physical condition	2	4	5
• Alternative locations	4	2	5
Total Raw Score	**23**	**21**	**35**

We showed the mythical Location "C" to illustrate what the score would be for an ideal location. Disregarding "C" and all things being equal (meaning that each attribute was equally important to you), you would choose Location "A" since it is nearly 10 percent better than Location "B" and is 66 percent of the unattainable mythical place. But all things are never equal. Notice that some attributes are obviously more important than others, but how much more? How could we quantify this qualitative issue? We have to weight each attribute against the others.

We do this by first ranking the attributes from most important to least. This makes rating them easier. Suppose you rank them like this.

1) Length of lease
2) Condition
3) Cost
4) Transportation
5) Local vendors
6) Alternative locations
7) Work force

These rankings are easier to make if you first pick the most important, then the least important, working your way to the middle. At this point you haven't said how much more important Item 1 is over Item 2, just that it is relatively more important than the next one.

The next step is matching numbers to your personal feelings of relativity. Again, the number system you use is immaterial, but suppose we stick with a rating of 1 to 5. If you had a longer list of attributes, you might choose a rating system of 1 to 10. Next, assign a rating of 5 to your most important attribute and a rating of 1 to the least. By that measure, "length of lease" gets a 5.0 and "work force" gets a 1.0. Then, look at the second most important attribute, condition. How much less important is it than length of lease? This is where your personal feelings are supposed to get quantified, not ignored. Based on your bad experience with poorly maintained property and the importance avoiding facility problems during start-up, you place a pretty high weight on the condition attribute. You could give it the same rating as the cardinal attribute if you wanted to. Instead you give it a 4.5, indicating that it isn't as important as the length of lease, but nearly so. You continue rating each subsequent attribute until you get to the bottom. If there is too large a jump between the next-to-the-last and the last attribute, you may want to go back and adjust your ratings. Suppose you come out with this rating.

RANK	ATTRIBUTE	RATING
1)	Length of lease	5.0
2)	Condition	4.5
3)	Cost	4.0
4)	Transportation	3.0
5)	Local vendors	2.5
6)	Alternative locations	2.0
7)	Work force	1.0

Now, you want to normalize the ratings, that is make them add up to 1.0 rather than 22.0. You do this by adding the ratings and then dividing each attribute rating by the total (e.g., $5 \div 22 = 0.23$ for the first attribute). The reason for doing this will be apparent soon. We promise.

RANK	ATTRIBUTE	RATING	NORMALIZED
1)	Length of lease	5.0	0.23
2)	Condition	4.5	0.20
3)	Cost	4.0	0.18
4)	Transportation	3.0	0.14
5)	Local vendors	2.5	0.11
6)	Alternative locations	2.0	0.09
7)	Work force	1.0	0.05
	Total	**22.0**	**1.00**

So far, you've quantified your feelings about the importance of each attribute to your final decision. You will take these weighting factors and multiply them by the original, unweighted ratings you gave each alternative. For example, transportation's rating at Location "A" is $5 \times 0.14 = 0.70$.

Weight	Attribute	LOCATION A	LOCATION B	LOCATION C
0.14	• Transportation	0.70	0.28	0.70
0.05	• Work force	0.10	0.20	0.25
0.18	• Lease cost	0.54	0.54	0.90
0.23	• Lease length	0.36	0.92	1.15
0.11	• Proximity to vendors	0.55	0.22	0.55
0.20	• Physical condition	0.40	0.80	1.00
0.09	• Alternative locations	0.36	0.18	0.45
	Total Weighted Score	**3.01**	**3.14**	**5.00**

By weighting the attributes the new score indicates that you should change your mind and choose Location "B" over "A". It is about 4 percent "better".

But your job isn't finished. Remember, we've cautioned several times before about taking models at face value. You can't. The implication that this decision model forecasts the best option is false. Like any tool, it's more important to know what it can't do than what it can do. The questions you have to ask include: What caused the preference to change from Location "A" to Location "B"? Is a 4 percent difference important, or are we essentially talking coin-flip here? If it is a coin-flip, what's the next important attribute we haven't listed or don't want to—perhaps the distance from our house to the new facility? Are the weights right? Are the ratings and rankings right? How much of a change in our ratings would cause the decision to flip again? The power of this decision tool is not that it makes the decision for you, but that it illustrates subjective considerations, helping you avoid or at least uncover decision errors and biases presented in the previous chapter.

COMPLICATIONS SET IN

The decision matrix ignores one unpleasant complication. Decisions are problematic because they involve uncertainty, and the decision matrix implies that the outcome of your decision is certain. It tackles the question of how to value outcomes, not how to handle the uncertainty. It helps order your preferences logically and systematically; however, it asks you to state the outcome of a future decision as a certainty when, in fact, you can't be certain. In the case of choosing the location for your next distribution warehouse, we rated the two alternatives by assuming the predicted outcome was certain. For example, when we rated each alternative on the "physical condition" attribute, we said that Location "B" was in better shape than Location "A". (Location "B" had a rating of 4; "A" had a rating of 2.) In fact, we predicted that B was 100 percent better than A. We don't know that for a fact; that's just an expression of our relative feelings about the physical condition of these two locations. We may have inspected the properties and even hired a building inspector. Nevertheless, we are quantifying our belief of how each stacks up against the other. For all we know Location "B" might have a latent electrical problem, which burns the place down after we move in. The decision matrix papers over the role of uncertainty in decision-making, but it's a good compromise between just musing aloud and building a model that includes the probability of fires caused by hidden electrical faults in buildings less than five years old.

There is, however, one more decision tool that you might want to use to model your probablistic forecast of uncertain events. While knowing the potential effects of hidden defects may not be a cost-effective use of your time, you might want to model the effect uncertainty has on your decision to sign a long- or short-term lease.

DID YOU REMEMBER TO WATER THE DECISION TREE?

Decision trees are the classical tool of technical staffs dedicated to solving sophisticated decision questions. These tools lend themselves to modeling probablistic outcomes that have monetary impact, but they can also be applied to nonmonetary outcomes as long as you can quantify your preference for one outcome over another. They are supposedly used by industries that regularly make large capital investments that hinge on future, uncertain events. Natural resource development, like mineral prospecting and hydroelectric projects, are paradigm investments for which decision trees are used to illustrate the impact of such uncertain events as future political climate, product cost, and expenses. Companies that play those games know that their assessments of the likely outcomes of these attributes have a considerable impact on their decision to invest. Like all models, this tool doesn't give a "Go" or "No-Go" answer. Rather, it shows how *estimates* of uncertainty might affect the decision. It is a way to test the sensitivity of your decision to the amount of uncertainty in the future outcome of that decision.

We omit all of the preliminary work necessary for a solid foundation in the use of decision trees because that's not what we're after. The most complicated tree you will ever draw will have four branches at most. Many times you won't even "solve" the decision tree, but instead you will use it to illustrate the structure of the problem. What every decision-maker needs is a grasp of the concepts—a simple example to come back to when you have a real-life problem to solve. If you need a better understanding of this tool so that you can communicate with experts who do this for a living, refer to the appendix for an appropriate reference.

Let's return to the question of which location you should lease for your distribution warehouse. Let's say that the landlord at your preferred site surprises you and makes you a double-sided offer. You can either lease the property for six months for $10,000 per month with a $1,000 escalator at each six-month anniversary for a maximum of two years, or you can sign a two-year lease at a flat

$10,000 per month. Which one you choose depends on your estimate of the chance your warehouse will be successful.

Figure 13.1 shows the basic decision. The two-year fixed lease will cost you $240,000. The six-month lease with the escalator will cost $276,000 over two years. If you remain for at least two years, you'd be $36,000 richer if you take the long-term lease. However, suppose you think there is a "high probability" that your distribution center will fail, and under such circumstances the potential $36,000 savings has to be balanced against your possible losses connected with getting out of a two-year lease. You need to know the effect of this uncertainty on your decision.

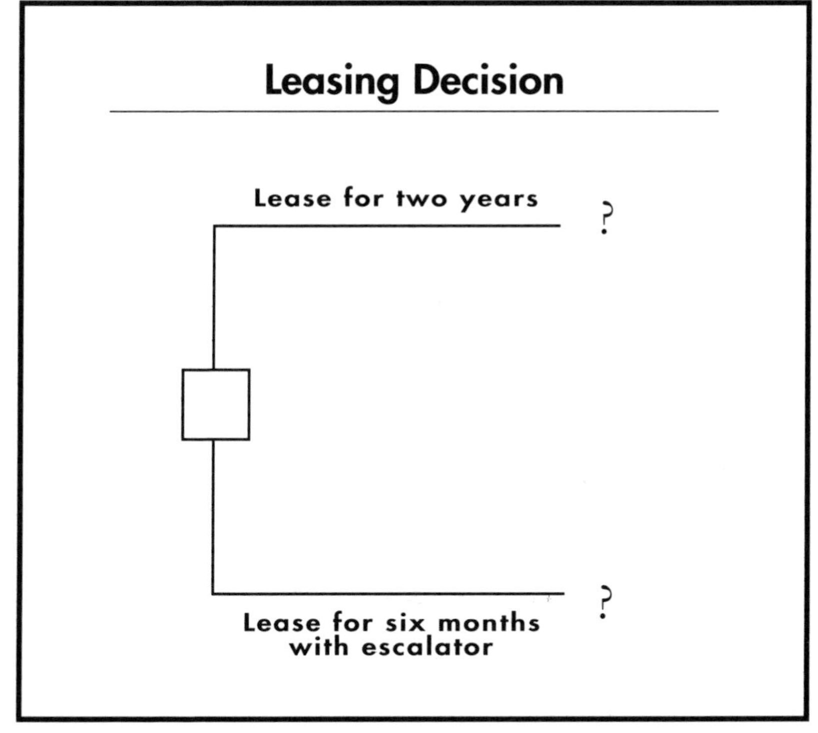

Figure 13.1

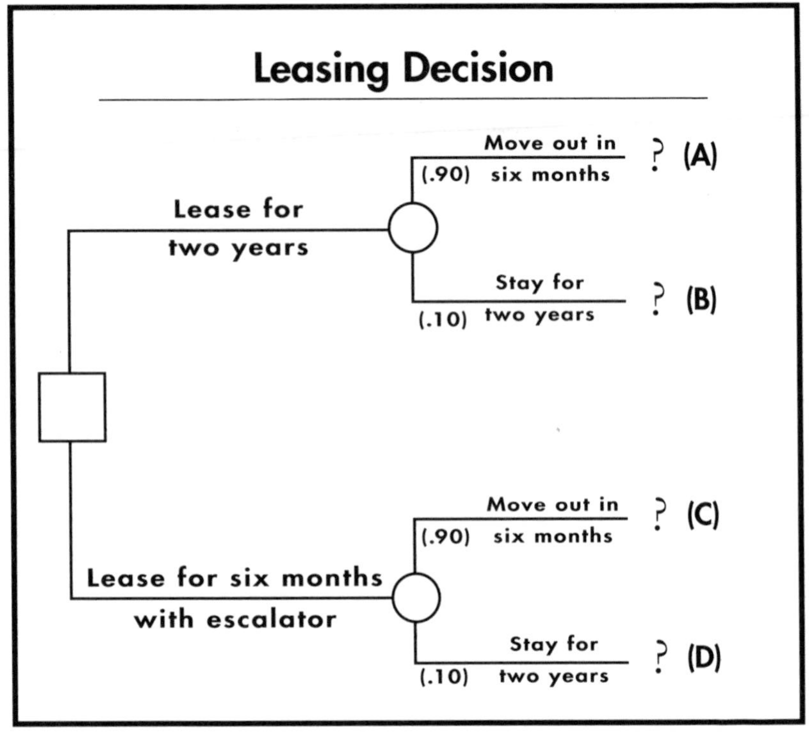

Figure 13.2

Figure 13.2 takes you through the first uncertain outcome. Regardless of which lease you take, the question remains, "What are the chances that the warehouse will last past six months?" To simplify the analysis, we'll assume that if it lasts six months, it will last two years. You assign the probability that it will close in six months as 90 percent; the chance that it will last two years is the balance or 10 percent. You have no quantitative information to help you set these probabilities. These probabilities merely reflect your confidence in your answer. How does one get to a 90 percent failure rate? First, without any information about the process under consideration, the chances of any two-outcome uncertainty is 50 percent, so that is where you start. Suppose you have had a bad track record opening new locations. That tends to make you pessimistic about the potential for the warehouse, but instead of avoiding all expansion possibilities, you want to ensure that all the decisions associated with your opening reflect this pessimism. Besides, you tell yourself, a 90 percent failure rate is not uncommon for new businesses of any kind, and each new location is essentially a new business.

Each branch of this decision tree has a monetary outcome. To calculate the top-most outcome, labeled (A) in Figure 13.2, you have to model one more uncertainty. Instead of suffering the complete loss of the cost of a two-year lease if you move out prematurely, you might be able to negotiate out of it or sublet. Suppose you think that you've got a 90 percent chance of getting away for the equivalent of one year's lease payment or $120,000. Your confidence comes from past experiences of negotiating out of leases gone bad. That means you figure you have a 10 percent chance of getting stuck for the complete $240,000. That could happen if the economy heads south in six months, making it impossible to sublet. Figure 13.3 shows how this additional uncertainty is added to the tree.

Outcomes "B", "C", and "D" shown in Figure 13.2 are straight-forward. If you stay for two years under the long-term contract, you'll pay $240,000. If you move out after six months under the short-term contract, you'll pay $60,000; while if you stay two years, you'll pay $276,000. But none of these outcomes are certain. To calculate the value of a branch on a decision tree, you multiply the outcome's value by the probability that the outcome will occur. The cost of the decision to lease for two years is $142,800; the cost of the decision to accept the short-term lease is $81,600 (see Figure 13.3 for these calculations). It's obvious that you should go with the short-term lease.

Or is it? The power of a decision tree is not that it can predict which alternative is more attractive, but that it shows the effect of your *assumed* probabilities on your decision. We always like to play with the probabilities to determine at what point a decision will flip. We then ask ourselves, "How close are we to that flip point, and how can we get more information to improve our risk assessment?"

Let's assume that you feel confident of your chances of negotiating out of the two-year lease (90 percent), but you're not so confident of your assessment that you'll be closing the warehouse in six months. A simple algebraic solution shows that the flip point for uncertainty is 33 percent. That is if you were to assess your chances of moving out at 33 percent or less, then going with the two-year lease is better than going with the short-term lease. Figure 13.4 illustrates this flip point. Unless you can come up with convincing data that erases your initial pessimism about the project and since the model is relatively insensitive to the possibility of moving out early, you'd probably stick with your original decision to sign a short-term lease, even

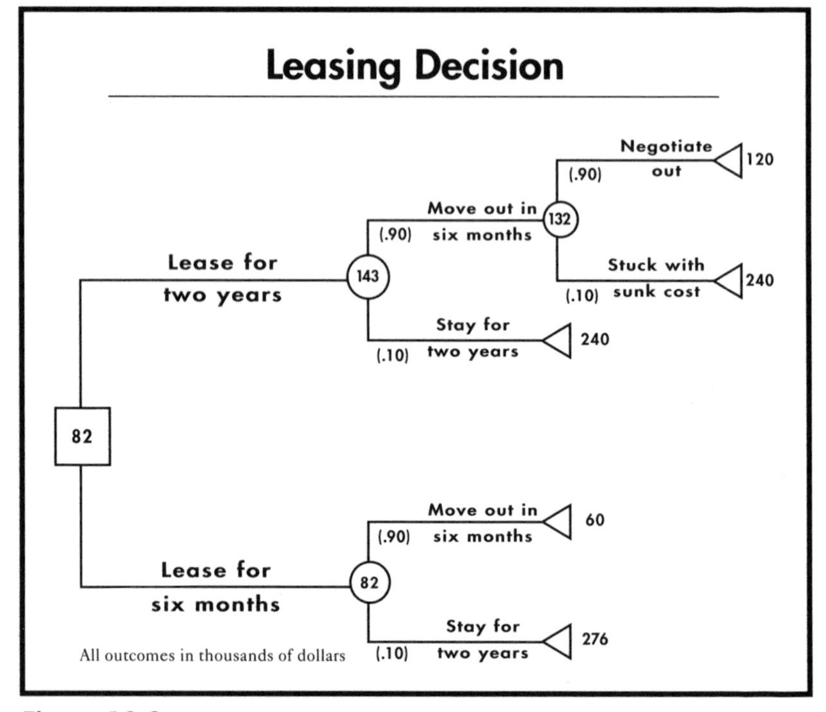

Figure 13.3

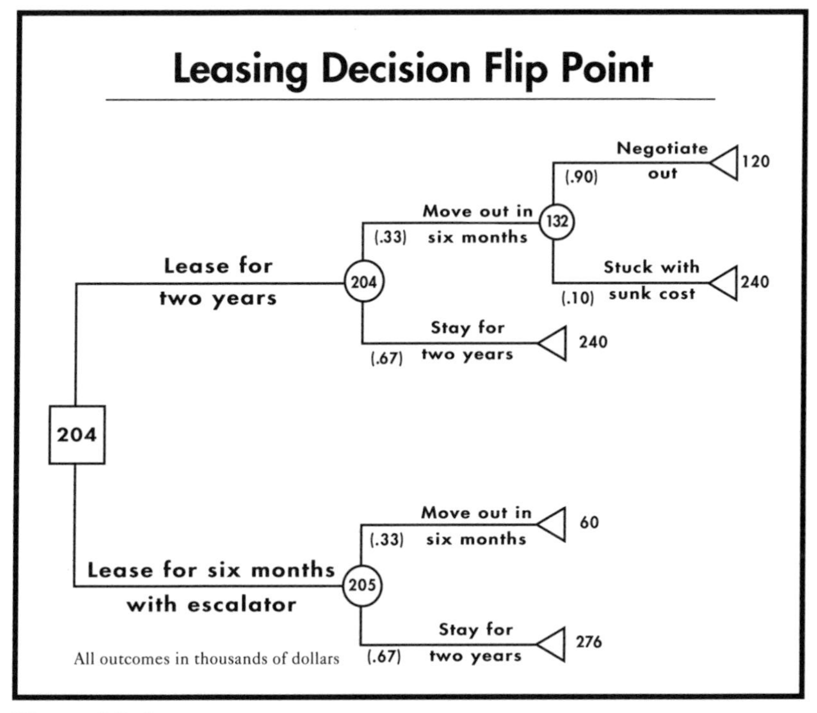

Figure 13.4

though it will cost more if the distribution center is successful.

Decision trees have the knack of injecting reality into business decisions that have become overwhelmed by overly optimistic forecasts. Expansion projects like this example tend to build momentum and are pushed along by groupthink and honoring sunk costs. Opening a branch location is a typical one where enthusiasm on the ground is crucial if you are going to improve the odds for success. This enthusiasm has to be tempered when looking at limiting the risks associated with the commitment to move ahead.

Again, no decision tool should be used exclusively. For instance, in this example you need to apply mini-max thinking if you decide that your initial pessimism was unwarranted. Suppose your sales force comes in with fantastic forecasts and a survey saying that the new location will be a hit. You have a chance to make an easy $36,000 by taking the longer lease. However, you have to think about minimizing your maximum regret. You may rather forego the possibility of getting $36,000 in order to minimize your maximum regret of being stuck with an empty warehouse and a commitment of $240,000, even if the possibility of that outcome now seems remote. Mini-max solutions are even more appropriate when the decision you face is fairly unique for you. If you were opening new locations every two weeks, then you'll have plenty of opportunities to take advantage of the odds in your favor. If opening a new location is a rare event, then you want to avoid gambler's ruin—the distinct possibility that even if the long-term odds are in your favor, your early play will be peppered with a string of bad luck.

DECISIONS ARE OPTIONAL

The last decision tool we want to explore is option-thinking. In the previous example, we mentioned that mini-max thinking could help you avoid a worst-case situation. Another way of looking at the extra $36,000 you'd spend on the short-term lease is to classify it as the cost of an option. An option is a investment that allows you to make an investment later (or conversely to avoid making an investment). Conventional options are financial instruments that allow the owner of the option to buy or sell a stock at a given price before a certain future date. Options come in other forms: You can negotiate an option allowing you to buy a certain piece of land at a certain price in the future. The buyer of an option isn't forced to buy or sell; he simply has the option to do so for a specified period. In our example, you could look at the additional $36,000 you will pay with the short-term lease as the price of an option that allows you to avoid an empty warehouse and a negative cash flow of $240,000. It is an option because you may not need it. You may find yourself staying in the facility for two-years under the short-term lease and not need the protection of the option.

Translating investment decisions into options is coming into its own, but option structures are more difficult to state and understand than other decision models, like decision trees, that imply a fixed answer. However, with a little ingenuity, most decisions can be coached in the language of options. Take the familiar decision to invest in a new machine. Suppose you can buy one large machine with a certain fixed output or three smaller machines whose total production equals the larger machine. Buying and operating the larger machine is less expensive than buying the three smaller machines. If you believe that you can load the larger machine, then the choice is obvious. However, the decision is not without uncertainty. How certain are you that you will be able to load the large machine? In this case the additional, incremental cost of buying and operating three smaller machines rather than one large one can be seen as the price of an option. The option allows you to adjust your production to meet the actual demand, thus avoiding having a less-than-100%-loaded monster machine. Your option also includes the opportunity, but not the obligation, to sell the excess productive capacity if your forecasted demand is less than the three small machines. Because of the uncertainty in your forecast and your ability to see the decision as an option (rather than a loss), you may indeed decide to go with the more expensive alternative of three small machines. The transformation of a decision into the terms of an option gives you another perspective on decision-making and provides another avenue to avoid decision errors presented in the previous chapter.

INTO THE BREACH

The most useful idea in this whole chapter is that you'll go far if all you do is use a pencil and paper to arrange and cultivate your thoughts, eliminate alternatives, search for obvious dominate strategies, and avoid common decision errors. If you use these tools to limit your downside risk, you will feel more comfortable with making difficult decisions, thereby moving forward more quickly and confidently because you know you did your best thinking. In the end, decision-making is a numbers game. The more decisions you make, the better the chance you'll make some good ones, especially if you ensure that the bad ones don't kill you.

14

Chapter 14

Duality

Art imitates life. In the 1993 movie *The Fugitive* Tommy Lee Jones played a U.S. Marshal charged with bringing in a convicted wife-killer, Dr. Richard Kimball, who escaped with another inmate. In one scene the posse corners an escapee who has taken one of the marshals hostage. Tommy Lee distracts the bad guy long enough to get in a few lucky shots. Later, when his associate tells Tommy Lee that he can't believe the marshal didn't try to negotiate first, Tommy Lee says in a slow whisper, "I . . . never . . . negotiate." This scene, along with other telling ones, builds the marshal's character into a straight shooter, so to speak.

As the movie builds towards its climax, the marshal displays fatherly attention to the well-being of his team, admits a few mistakes to his fellow posse members, and even shows conditional sympathy towards Dr. Kimball. Rather than detracting from the business-side of the marshal's character, this soft-side actually enhances the audience's appreciation of the marshal as a genuine person. Script writers call this character balance, and it is as necessary in the real world as it is in good storytelling. Successful managers from first-line supervisors to CEOs must master their dual role of leader and comrade.

DUALITY, A NECESSITY

The sixth fundamental skill of management is the ability to project this duality. It is a difficult capacity to develop; some say it is a talent. Many of us are familiar with inept managers, who were artificially harsh when the situation called for understanding, only to be overtly but disingenuously kind when trying to recover. We also have seen or heard about bosses who avoided confrontation like the plague and those who couldn't live without it. These people were struggling unsuccessfully with their duality.

To these managers the sensitivity training fads of the '90s were a disaster for various reasons. Being tough was out, being kind was in. Managers were to be more sensitive; employees were encouraged to be more assertive. In an attempt to re-educate old-style managers, those classified as too abrupt, blunt, or harsh were sent to charm school to knock off a few rough edges while employees enrolled in assertiveness training classes. These schools implied that changing management style was not unlike learning to get along with some of your in-laws. It might be distasteful at times, but in the interest of the family it was better to find a way to tolerate them. They claimed that the "new" management style was more professional, more acceptable, and more successful than the "old" way. No doubt the management education wave of the 2000s will swing towards toughness and responsibility and be dubbed something like the "Reality Management Movement (RMM)."

The content of these management re-education programs is immaterial because their objectives are inappropriate and unattainable. Except for the short-term damage done to participants doomed to fail and the waste of time and opportunity, these faddish re-education schools cannot change anything. By this point in this book, you know why: Changing something as personal and inseparable as management style is the most complex change initiative there is, subject to all of the problems we mentioned in the previous chapters discussing change. Whether we're trying to make managers more "people-oriented" or more "business-oriented," the results are similar. Back on the job a few weeks or at the most a few months, the "bad" manager begins to backslide. It's agonizing to his subordinates as well. They can tell the manager is trying very hard to become a "better manager," only to become frustrated by the difficulty of trying to be someone he's not. Managers who were classified as "too tough" find that no one believes their metamorphosis is real. Those managers who were told they were "too undemanding" never become comfortable with asserting themselves.

When the principles of change dynamics are applied, it becomes obvious that a company program for management re-education is universally unworkable in America. First, we have trouble getting past the first standard question, "Why change?" Very few managers, even those who are convinced that their style is the root of their company's problems, will be able to answer, "Why change?" unequivocally. Remember, this question is asked during the unfreezing stage and revisited continually, consciously or unconsciously, throughout the change process. Second, defining and justifying a company, division, or department change objective in terms of a personal change objective is very problematic: What's the cost? Where's the profit? How long will it take? How will we know when we're finished? Third, look at a typical force-field analysis of a personal change initiative (see Chapter 8). What are you going to show as forces encouraging and opposing change? How is an unbecoming management style a serious threat to survival? What's the source of disconfirming information? Can it be collaborated with external information? Are the external sources of disconfirming information strong, consistent, and insistent? Fourth and last, how are you going to measure change? Typically, management-style changeovers are justified on the basis of obvious-by-inspection, supposedly needing little project-specific economic justification. But as we've said before, in business, if you can't measure it, it doesn't exist.

We are not saying that changing management style is an inappropriate *change* objective. We're saying that it is an inappropriate *business* project. Few personal change projects are appropriate as company- or department-wide projects. How about undertaking a physical fitness change objective? An abstinence initiative? Why not put together a program to enhance management and employee spirituality? While some companies have embarked on these types of change initiatives, these programs are outside the *definition of a business* change program. They are inappropriate because they can't pass the tests of a business initiative. Of course, what employees or managers do on their own time isn't the company's business, and whether or not it is profitable to encourage private behavior by providing facilities for such activities is a very different question left as an exercise.

DUALITY REQUIRES CONSISTENCY

If duality is a fundamental management skill independent of style, how do we develop it? First, we have to have a better handle on the nature of duality, and second, we have to find tools to help us reinforce that nature. ***Duality*** is a skill that good managers have for appearing simultaneously as a leader and as a comrade. Therefore, duality is a personal skill, apparent both in group settings and one-on-one. If we are to reinforce duality, we have to have a strategy for both situations.

Duality was listed as the last of the six fundamental skills because it is enhanced by the other fundamental skills: profit fixation, techno-literacy, change dynamics insight, policy and procedure comprehension, and decision theory knowledge. Having a profit-focus helps improve your consistency, thereby enhancing your leadership presence. Organizational psychologists have various competing theories about what makes a leader, but most agree that people universally respond to consistency. That's natural. Without consistency, followers have trouble forming pictures (i.e., gestalts) consistent with their leader's. Furthermore, followers seldom get closure if their leader, with little preparation or forewarning, continually changes focus. Understanding how people change and the role that awareness plays in that process improves the personal side of your duality. Additionally, while people like to like their bosses, they're more impressed by bosses who are technically competent than those who are good storytellers. The techniques of good decision theory add to your caché as a competent group leader, and understanding your role in policy and procedure formation ensures that you intervene at appropriate places and times.

The bulk of this book has been taken up with ways to develop a balanced portfolio of business management skills. Those skills lend themselves to objective measurement and can be improved using practiced methods. Duality depends on developing personal relationships in a business environment and is less conducive to formulaic solutions. Nevertheless, there are a few ideas that might help improve this last and most enigmatic fundamental management skill.

SHARED DECISION-MAKING

Bosses always complain that being at the top is lonely. They say they have no one inside the company to talk to, and when they do confide, they feel that they pay for it. They find that more is made of their inquiries and questions. Instead of getting a handle on a problem, they find themselves inadvertently feeding the rumor mill. In retrospect, this syndrome reflects a different kind of inconsistency on a manager's part. In addition to being inconsistent when it comes to goals, objectives, policy and procedure, managers can be inconsistent with the way they include or exclude people from their decisions. The balance between being seen as a leader and being seen as a comrade is influenced by the topics you reserve for yourself and those you share with others. If you are consistent about what topics are appropriate for each forum, you find that people respect and understand your duality.

In the 1979 film *All That Jazz* the protagonist gets up every morning, prepares himself for the day in the same way, and before going out looks in the mirror, puts on a smile and says, "Show Time!" Likewise, every time you are at work as a manager, some part of you says, "Show time!" You know that someone will be watching and listening, trying to extract as much meaning as they can from your mood, your demeanor, your little asides. Too many managers want to forget that they, more than anyone else, must think before they speak, verify that what they've said was fully understood, and recover if they've mis-spoken. Someone once said the mark of a professional is doing your best even when you don't feel like it, and many times managers don't particularly feel like being "on". They want to let their hair down; they want to have a few friends on the inside.

People want their leaders to be human, too, but their allowance is not as great as it is for themselves. What a leader such as yourself chooses to discuss freely must follow a pattern. If one time you muse about the company's finances and the next you treat it as a state secret, you'll be seen for what you appear to be: an untrustworthy confidant. If you encourage people to tell you what they don't like about the company and then don't do anything about their complaints, then you'll be seen as what you appear to be: disingenuous. If you ask them their opinion about a particularly difficult decision affecting them and then make a decision that totally ignores their input, you'll be seen as what you appear to be: conniving. Never mind that you're none of these. Your actions speak louder than words.

THE INCLUSION TREE

The prerogatives of leadership include the responsibility for the decision when it's all said and done. Your constant dilemma is that you can't make robust decisions without getting information from people around you, but as soon as you engage someone you have to ensure closure. The dilemma is solved if you have a strategy for inclusion. We call it an ***inclusion tree***, a reference to the decision tree presented in Chapter 13. You must ask yourself these questions when deciding whom to include or exclude:

1) ***Does the decision lend itself to analysis, or are we talking about preference?***
   It makes no sense to include other people's opinion if the final decision rests on your preference. Be brutally honest with your answer to this question. If you consistently lie to yourself and say, "Yes, this decision lends itself to analysis, and I need other people's input," and then do what you want anyway, the people around you will learn to withhold information routinely. Then, when you really need their input, you won't get it. On the other hand, if you include people in your decision only when you really need objective input, they will be more prone to share their knowledge.

2) ***If the decision lends itself to analysis, will the answer be enhanced if I include other people's input?***
   The glib answer is, "You always should include other people's input. You're a cretin if you don't." We disagree. In some cases you don't have time

to include other points of view. In some cases the analysis is simple and direct. In some cases security of the decision requires limited distribution (i.e., notification on a need-to-know basis). If it's more important to protect the decision than it is to improve its quality, then make the decision yourself or with limited input. Some complex change initiatives require the agreement of many people and alignment of forces for change (e.g., introduction of a new product line). On the other hand, some complex change initiatives require the agreement of few people and require a high level of security (e.g., reducing headcount during a severe recession).

3) ***If I need other people's input, whom do I include to ensure a good decision?***
While this question is stated as inclusive, deciding whom to exclude is actually harder. Most managers find it easy to include and routinely find that they've included too many nonessential people. In any case the reasons for inclusion or exclusion must be shared with those involved. If people think they should be included and are not, they react badly if they aren't told why. Suppose you exclude someone because you don't trust him to be objective, even though he may have a valuable point of view. You've got to be honest with him. Let him present his case. Let him participate in a conditional basis, if you must, but don't make a big mystery out of it. Intrigue is good for Sherlock Holmes, but it has no place when you're concerned with the quality of a decision. On the other hand, you may have to include diverse, closed-minded opinions if implementing the proposed decision requires consensus. Again, it

makes no sense to pretend that differences don't exist. They do, and you must address them up front.

LIMITING INCLUSION

This last point brings up a couple of issues that must be emphasized. The trend has been to extol the virtue of embracing as many diverse opinions and ideas when searching for a solution to a problem. This inclusion tree leans against that wind. In our pursuit of improving the quality of decisions by widening the information net, we have ignored the importance of context in shaping an inclusion strategy. Taking an example from our files, a company that designs and installs architectural accessories decided to embark on a team-based, problem-solving program. With the president's approval the outside consultant encouraged middle management to brainstorm the problems needing attention, and they chose salary administration and fringe benefits. They drew Pareto diagrams, assembled lists of information they needed, and assigned work goals. The wheels fell off the program for several reasons, but a climb through the inclusion tree would have prevented the disaster in the first place. Salary administration topics usually require limited participation to ensure the security of the process. Otherwise, expectations rise, personal agendas are aired, and forces opposing change built prematurely and fatally. Besides that, the president would have answered "NO!" to the second inclusion tree question had it been asked.

The second point is usually avoided in polite management discussions: the role of conflict and employment termination in improvement programs. Supposedly, companies are enlightened places where people spend stress-free lives improving themselves and their companies. Termination is the mark of a weak manager unable to help a troubled employee and is a symptom of Neanderthal employment practices. Not necessarily. Conflict is a natural state when two or more people hold dear opposing opinions that cannot be resolved without one side or the other or both changing an essential principle of their understanding of how things work. Conflict is the essence of any change initiative. Whether those conflicts can be resolved in the time available determines whether or not one side or the other can remain in the group. The importance of the required change and of the relative strengths of the conflicting ideas is left on the manager's desk to decide the next move. Some changes cannot be left to eventual resolution, and termination is the only solution.

DUALITY, A STATE OF MIND

What's important when considering the inclusion tree is not the absolute issue at hand but its relationship to others. Deciding when to include or exclude other people in your decisions reflects both personal choice and the company's "culture". The important ingredients are that management be consistent, that shared decisions have the same relative importance, and that those decisions left to the prerogative of leadership are likewise related. If you treat the assignment of weekend duty as one requiring limited input but the assignment of company cars as a group decision, it will be hard for people to understand how inclusion works.

As you grow accustomed to recognizing instances of duality, you'll see that it takes many forms. A rock-and-roll story shows how good managers of all persuasions recognize duality's importance. In the late 1980s the ex-Beatle Paul McCartney produced a documentary of his American tour. At this point in his career he also produced his own music, so he had a million and one things to look after and about the same number of problems to solve. A telling point in the film came when the interviewer was talking with the members of his band. One said that when

Paul showed up at rehearsals and sound checks he never talked about the business side of the tour. All he shared was his music and his excitement about the tour. Paul's duality was a refreshing and uncommon trait, and for the music side of the business a critical skill if band members were to concentrate on their part of the tour's success. Paul knew this, and both avoided including them in issues for which they had nothing to add (finance and front office operations) and instead nurtured their awareness of issues for which they had substantial impact (manufacturing). The band also recognized the situation and respected Paul in some ways more for the management skills he brought to the organization than his musical abilities, which were indeed awesome.

Earlier in this book we mentioned in passing that all types of management styles can be successful. Dysfunctional management is not a problem of style but one of consistency, predictability, and trueness—trueness meaning being true to your natural character. In the end, that sincerity is the source of your individual duality.

15

Chapter 15

The Fad Parade

The central premise of this book is that general management, like any profession, rests on certain fundamental skills and that much of what ails dysfunctional companies derives both from our inattention to these skills and our avaricious taste for the latest Management Fad of the Month. So far in this book we've taken apart empowerment and team-building and took a swipe at inappropriate application of technology. In this chapter we'll gather together some of the more popular management fads of the 1990s and see if we can make any sense of them.

Our treatment will seem a little harsh, especially if we've picked on one of your favorites. We have no malice toward any one fad. We believe that all of them are universally flawed, not because of their basic premises but because their practitioners tend to elevate one fundamental over all others. We want to show how the complete set of fundamental management skills presented in this book, along with a little common sense, can reveal that the emperor has no clothes.

But before we go about trashing some the currently popular management fads, we have to answer two common questions. First, given that most American products built in the 1990s were better than those built in the 1970s, shouldn't the management initiatives associated with this era share some of the credit for this success? Second, how can so many people be so wrong?

While we agree that products built today are, in general, better than those built 20 years ago, it is also true that products built in the 1890s were substantially better than those built in the 1870s. That era was able to improve on product design, manufacturing methods and organizational structure without the benefit of management fads. Therefore, how much of the improvement we saw during our lifetimes should we attribute to the various late 20th century management fads? More to the point, isn't it just as likely that we would have had more improvement had our taste for management fads been subdued? We'd like to quote from a recent study of the impact of management fads on the American economy that shows that fads have had a negative impact on our economy. But we are resigned to the fact that if such a study existed, it would be flawed because no one can predict the path not taken. In the end you have to judge for yourself whether or not fads, per se, add to our GNP. It is an article of faith, based on personal experience, extensive observation and ruthless comparative analysis, that fads have little redeeming value.

The second question implies that mass delusion is a rare event and that a measure of an idea is its popularly. World history is full of instances where mass delusion was very commonplace. In the late 1600s the European aristocracy was caught up in the Tulip Craze, a speculative bubble that saw the price of tulip bulbs exceed thousands of dollars a piece in today's dollars. Among those caught by the market's eventual collapse was Sir Isaac Newton. More recently, hundreds of millions of dollars were invested in the early 1980s in the domestic oil and gas business based on the widely-accepted forecast of $100 per barrel oil and $10 per thousand cubic feet of gas. Since then, the market price of oil has rarely gone above $20 per barrel and gas above $2 per thousand cubic feet. On a sadder and recurring note, popular belief is the root of genocide. Hitler's *Mein Kampf* was a worldwide best seller and formed the basis of one of our more horrific examples of the error and terror of the masses.

On the other hand, as we have pointed out elsewhere in this book, some people somewhere at some time get some benefit from pursuing the latest fad. But a review of the drivers of change indicates that almost any management initiative would have worked given the unrelated but fortuitous circumstances of those who succeed. It's not the fad; it's the intent and talent of people who want to change. It is our experience that most management fads are born *after* the first mover moved. First movers rarely interpret what they've done as an innovative management initiative, but rather as a response to pressing needs. Only after the business press picks up on a particularly good business success story does a management fad spring up around a set of practices identified with the latest corporate hero. Whether or not other people can benefit from these collected and associated practices depends more on good luck and dedicated management than on the power of the subsequent management fad.

REENGINEERING AND TECHNOLOGY

For our first analysis we'll look at reengineering since at the time this book was written it had just entered intensive care and slow death was at hand. Reengineering is a paradigm for the business fad movement, not only because its fast rise and short history were so typical of management fads but also because it championed a cherished myth about the power of technology.

Reengineering had two advantages over competing fads of the day: fortuitous timing and superficial understanding. As far as timing, it was introduced during a coincidental spasm of wide-spread, widely-reported lay-offs (euphemistically called right-sizing) that was thundering across the American business landscape. Reengineering promised that your company could do the same amount of work with fewer people, but only if it followed certain principles of management and systems design, dubbed ***reengineering***. Superficial understanding came into play and contributed to its success as a business fad because managers implementing reengineering neglected to read the seminal book, *Reengineering the Corporation*, by James Champy and Michael Hammer. Central to the authors' thesis, and indivisible from it, was the role of technology in successful reengineering programs, particularly computer technology. In the end, reengineering became a buzz-word rationale for mindless downsizing. The point is not that downsizing was or was not needed; it is that superficial managers, who only read the book reviews, directed their staffs to "reengineer" the company by cutting staff some arbitrary amount. The confusion over what reengineering was and was not became so laughable by 1995 that many confused it with TQM—an older, more resilient fad that we will examine later in this chapter.

Every management fad has a quick-fix theme. For reengineering, technology was the holy grail. Earlier in Chapter 6 we said that the impact of new technology on business transformation has remained about the same throughout recorded history. While the technology we fixate on today is the computer, such machines are by no means the only new technology presenting opportunities for profit. However, computers seem to have captured the imagination of pop culture journalists in a way not possible for plastics, metals, ceramics, and packaging materials, all examples of emerging technologies that may improve our standard of living by lowering costs.

The computer industry has done an extremely fine job of selling their technology as not only essential to survival for all industries, but practically as essential as air and water is to life. However, you don't have to dig too deeply to find disconfirming information concerning the value of computer technology in running businesses. Before record downsizing hit American business in the early- to mid-1990s, economists were perplexed by consistently repeatable numbers showing that the productivity of American office workers was not increasing, despite the billions of dollars spent on automating overhead functions. There were bright spots here and there and good stories to tell, but no matter how it was measured, white-collar productivity didn't seem to get the same boost from computers as the factory worker did. What were people doing with such large capital investments in the front office?

The central problem with employing computer technology in the work place and, therefore, with reengineering in general is that managers approving the implementation of the technology give too little thought about how it will change the way people work. Without any concrete idea of which jobs will change, where the efficiencies will come, and exactly how people will do their jobs after the new computer system is up and running (as opposed to how they did it the day before), costs do not fall. Rather, many technological applications lead to additional features, which upon examination add little value. "You will be able to get your reports on a daily basis instead of weekly," you're told. What good is that if you pile them up on your desk and continue to review them on a weekly basis anyway? "You'll be able to model the market much more accurately," you're promised. Says who? We don't even understand how our models work today. Why should we pay more attention to one generated by a machine when it can't even predict the past? "With E-mail we'll be able to improve communications," you're told. We're covered up by meaningless memos and weighed down by voice mail already. Sure, I need another way to avoid talking to someone directly.

All of these snide remarks cut to the quick. Applied technology requires a lot of pre-installation thinking about how the technology will *improve profitability* and change work routines. For example, suppose your product is metal-based, and you're exploring the possibility of replacing some of the metal with plastic. Would you call in a few plastic vendors, get their ideas, and then order a couple of tons on the bet that your operations staff could figure out how to use it? Of course not. Then, why are computers and computer systems bought that way? Our experience is that rigorous operational analysis and cost justifications for computer investments are seldom done because many general managers are illiterate when it comes to systems design and fundamental problem-solving. Few seem eager to learn, and vendors capitalize on this attitude.

A good example of how inattentive use of technology can overwhelm techno-illiterate managers is the problem of excessive E-mail. In the mid-1990s general managers realized that E-mail provided new ways for diverse groups to communicate, especially those whose work was interdependent but separated by thousands of miles and tens of hours. Regular mail was too slow, overnight charges too expensive. E-mail provided the right mix of service and cost. However, eventually E-mail traffic grew so fast that getting through your daily E-mail before the end of the day became problematic. Messages started piling up, unanswered. E-mailers began habitually telephoning or faxing their intendents to tell them that an E-mail message was waiting for them. The conventional answer to this emerging problem was to use technology to rescue what was basically a non-technological problem. Applying declassified intelligence processing techniques, software developers promised programs that would digest E-mail messages and, using "artificial intelligence," produce summaries so that you could decide which messages needed to be read in full and which you could, presumably, just pretend that you read before you junked them.

The solution would be absurd if it were not so shocking that many managers actually thought that this was a good solution to the problem. The real problem was not with the receivers' inability to read their mail; it was with the senders' inability to write. When our business skills become so poor that we can't depend on people to write cogent summaries of their own work, when we become such poor teachers that people cannot stop themselves from using the word "subsequent" seven times in two pages, when we become so lame that we lose sight that general management—not technology—is responsible for designing command-and-control systems to regulate communications traffic, it's time for us to go home.

The problem with uncritical application of computer and information technology is both profound and complex. The only way we are going to overcome it is by becoming sensitive to it, not becoming anti-technology rubes. Being anti-technology is as lame-brained as embracing technology thoughtlessly. The questions you ought to ask each time a new computer technology or any new technology is proposed is, "How will this investment change the way we work? How will that change make us money?"

Many times some dimensions of new technology can be subtle but as potent as the obvious ones. This book is a perfect example. The obvious impact of computer technology is that we could not have written and published it in the 1970s, even though the principles and problems we repeat here existed then. Twenty years ago the cost of producing this book would have prevented the authors from even thinking about publishing it without financial backers willing to take a chance on a contrarian idea. By the 1990s, the computer lowered the cost of production, and writing a book became possible. That is the obvious story. The not-so-obvious but more interesting story of applied technology is hidden back in the print shop, specifically something called typesetting.

Typesetting is a craft. It involves choosing compatible fonts, type styles, page presentation, and solving a myriad of problems with word-wrap, page breaks, and set-up. With the advent of publishing software, direct-to-film processes, high-resolution laser drafts, and other processing techniques, the traditional role of the typesetter in building a book has been discarded, one limb at a time. During this transformation, the collective, integrative knowledge of the typesetter has been replaced by amateurs who, instead of offering measured solutions, generate endless versions for consideration by an uninformed customer. The rules of presentation, learned by the typesetter over a lifetime of work, has slipped away unnoticed. Today many people in the publishing and printing trades look at you quizzically when you ask who the typesetter will be. They don't consider typesetting relevant to the process anymore.

This is not merely a pining for the old days. The loss of craft is noticeable in many professions. If this loss had been a conscious decision that considered the impact of such a loss on the final product, then we have a planned event. But because technology is installed with little thought concerning where various value-added components reside and how they are applied, product deterioration is inevitable. Today, whole industries are waking up to find that their products have mysteriously become less than the sum of its parts.

We did not always share this feeling that applied technology can obliterate value-added craft but came to realize this over a ten-year period. The first we became aware of the potential loss of craft through applied technology was when we argued *against* the supposition that computer-aided drafting (CAD) would open drafting, architecture, engineering, and similar fields to mediocre and unworthy talents. What troubled a commentator of the time was her belief that one's ability to work the boards somehow reflected other associated skills that determined how good a practitioner a person would be. Her thought was that if someone were able to fake board work by using

CAD as a crutch, it would take longer to find him out, leading to lower, not higher productivity. Of course, her hypothesis was unprovable since she had to establish some causal link between drawing a pretty line and thinking about a pretty line.

Her argument was intriguing, but lead nowhere until we transformed it into a hypothesis about how increased efficiency provided by technology can lead to poorer output, not better. The hypothesis is rooted in human nature. If I can re-write a business letter almost (repeat: almost) effortlessly, I find myself spending less time composing than just spewing words out. After all, I know I can come back and dress it up later. The rub comes when you consider that a written word becomes an anchor. In the past, when re-writes were much more expensive, I took longer to think about what I wanted to say, how I wanted to say it, who my audience was, and whether a phone call would be more efficient. Reflection as part of the creative process is lost when word processing technology allows me to combine thinking about my communication problem and creating the vehicle at the same time. Whether the ability to think and create concurrently makes up for the lack of reflection probably depends on the activity. Some work will benefit, but some will come away worse for the new combination.

It occurred to us that what was bothering the anti-CAD Luddite wasn't fully formed at the time. But behind every opposing position is a reality that must be addressed. Before CAD-based engineering, a designer would spend more time sketching ideas and disregarding the more obvious dead-ends. He couldn't explore all the possibilities because full-blown, drawn, checked, and reviewed drawings were expensive. Instead, an experienced designer used his accumulated skill and knowledge to avoid dead-ends. CAD-based engineering may indeed represent a process in which the reflection of a craftsman is replaced by the ability to explore an increased number of possibilities. The question remains whether or not we understand that trade-off. In any case, in your everyday world you will develop better technology-based solutions if you keep in mind that technology is merely a fancy word for change.

If you don't struggle with its implications, technology becomes a fad itself. Stories abound how premier companies like Federal Express, American Airlines, *et al* used information technology in the 1980s and 1990s to their advantage. What's forgotten in the re-telling of the story is that their new technology was part of a coherent operational strategy that centered on that technology. Too many companies assign the care and feeding of new "technologies" to an existing function rather than looking at it as an integrative solution that remains the responsibility of general management.

THE KING OF CONFUSION: QUALITY IMPROVEMENT PROGRAMS

What would happen if the chairman of the board of Amalgamated Armtronics, a publicly-traded company with 20 billion dollars of yearly sales, sent out a press release saying that they were embarking on an innovative program that included such novel ideas as watching costs, protecting market share, and generally listening to customers? Your retort might be, "What have you been doing up to now? Ignoring costs, sales, and your customers?" Of course no one announces an improvement program that emphasizes normal business behavior. How is it then that companies routinely announce with pride that they are embarking on a "quality improvement program"? Was quality a feature ignored before and just now noticed? More likely, they are just aping the latest fad.

The first indication that quality improvement programs are destined for trouble is that their objective, ***quality***, is an undefinable term. Any effort aimed at improving quality runs into endless debates concerning what quality is and is not. This problem is so severe that leading practitioners always start their canned quality program by defining the term, only to be attacked by other equally-expert practitioners who loudly proclaim that their definition is better. This intellectual arm-wrestling sets the stage for continuous turmoil in the pre-packaged quality-improvement-program industry.

This problem will never be solved because all programs organized around quality themes harbor an inescapable paradox. Quality program advocates generally express the problem as one of definition, implying that inconvenient semantics lie at its roots. It is *not* a problem of semantics. It is much deeper and more profound than that. To understand how devastating this problem is you need to know something about a fascinating mathematical discovery called Godël's theorem. You don't need to know anything about math, either, to appreciate its implications.

Some biographers and historians say that the great philosopher and mathematician Bertrand Russell became clinically insane or at least a broken man because his life's work was negated by Godël's. If such a premier mind as Bertrand Russell can be crushed by this paradox, think what happens when mere mortals in the quality improvement industry find themselves floating in this same intellectual sea. Russell spent nearly 20 years of his life proving that mathematics was the one fundamentally pure science. He attempted to do this by showing that its foundation—logic—was consistent, coherent and self-sustaining. The hallmark of such a system is that it is free from paradox. ***Paradox*** in mathematics or any system appears when a statement is unprovable from within the system, but nonetheless true. We face paradox in many human endeavors, and some say that the power of the human mind is that it can cope with these unprovable truths. How we do this is still unknown and may be unknowable.

Mathematics was supposed to be free of paradoxes. Mathematicians assumed that every and all mathematical hypotheses can be proved either true or false, given enough time, insight and creativity. Russell wanted to prove this assumption. He wanted to prove that mathematics was unique in that it could support itself from within, exclusive of any help from an outside observer. This is not a trivial point. All science and rational human progress depended, as far as Russell was concerned, on mathematics having such a basis. It drove to the heart of the question whether mathematics existed as a universal truth or was a construct of the human mind.

In relation to our own daily lives, Russell's effort seems like entertainment for eggheads. We take for granted that math is math. Anywhere in the universe, two plus two equals four. Godël's theorem (called the Incompleteness Theorem for reasons which will become obvious) removed mathematics from the realm of truth and put it in the realm of faith. More than that, it removed any hope of escaping paradox in *any* system, whether it be math, physics, or quality. In essence, Godël said that any system built on a set of axioms (i.e., statements taken as true on their face) will have an indefinite number of statements that cannot be proven true or false, but are nonetheless true. Furthermore, this troubling feature remains no matter how many additional axioms you add in your effort to nail down "truth". The problem rests with nature's apparently self-referential nature.

The current and forever continuing problem with quality improvement programs is as close as most of us will get to see the effects of the Incompleteness Theorem. It is more obvious in the quality field than in mathematics because the self-referential nature of quality is not hidden beneath layers of thought but lies on the surface. Most of us use mathematics without becoming overwhelmed by this esoteric problem. Not so with practitioners of quality.

The very foundation of their work rests on the obvious self-referential concept of quality. We say something is a *quality* piece of work, or that it reflects *quality*, never worrying that we are referring to a concept that is unprovable but nonetheless true. We know that quality exists. If we were to remove the concept from our world, the world would be a very different place. But just because something like quality exists doesn't mean we are able to define it.

Before now, you may have been unaware of this small but significant tear in the fabric of the universe. Maybe you thought the problem was yours alone when you became vertiginous every time you did quality thinking about quality. But if you lose your balance when thinking about quality, think about the kinds of problems you'll have when a whole company takes up a program built on a self-referential concept. It invites chaos. Because of the limits of self-referentialism, we have to accept on faith that quality does exist. We can't define it sufficiently to say that we have a "quality improvement program" in place. That's somewhat equivalent to saying we have a "business program" in place.

This fatal flaw in quality systems development doesn't stop people from selling quality improvement programs, and 30 to 40 percent of targeted companies feel that they have accomplished something. In this practical, self-sustaining world of quality consultants, some experts limit their definition of quality to "conformance to requirements." This neat trick serves to convert a quality improvement program to a conformance-to-specification program. What is left out of this neat conversion is the troublesome fact that someone outside of the "quality system," but presumably having access to it, has to define what the requirements are. We assume that they depend on their own personal sense of what quality is. Some other practitioners attempt to solve the problem by assigning the responsibility of deciding what quality is to the customer. Aside from the fact that someone inside the company still has to interpret a customer's self-referential statements about quality, we will soon show you that in the case of quality the customer is not always right.

A favorite example of the complex and self-referential nature of quality shows up in the discussion of quality television. In the mid-1990s, when U.S. government funding of public television was in jeopardy, advertisements on the Public Broadcasting System included such quotable quotes as, "Public TV is Quality." Coincidentally, these ads ran the same time a commercial network was trumpeting that they were rated "Number One in Quality Television Programming," based on viewer polls used to set advertising rates. In the strange world of quality, both statements were true. Public TV has always claimed to be the quality network, presumably because low ratings indicate that high-brow programming appeals to a higher "quality" viewer. At least, that's what regular public television viewers like to think about themselves. On the other hand, the networks dismiss public television, rightly claiming that commercial television provides quality programming, presumably because more people watch it than public TV. The fact that both networks can rightly claim a quality product strongly implies that quality is an irrational and, therefore, inappropriate business initiative.

Feeling a little off balance now? This is the same feeling, but less intense, that overcomes anyone involved for any length of time in a quality program. It's the feeling that you're making progress only to find yourself at the same place you were earlier. Lots of scenery passed by, but all you've done is burned up some gas, depreciated your car a little more, and engaged in sometimes-boring, sometimes-interesting conversation. You still haven't made any money. That is not to say that some people, somewhere, sometime actually get value from a quality improvement program. They certainly aren't shy about sharing their success stories. But underneath the story is the truth that certain elements of their quality program were more successful than others. The successful elements are *always* the ones that fortuitously had a force-field profile (see Chapter 8) conducive to change at the time the program came along. The successful program elements fit well with existing and recognized operating problems. All the company needed was a methodology to convert the existing pent-up demand for change to action. The fact that the methodology was delivered under the cover of a fad was coincidental to what really happened at ground zero.

Ultimately, quality is not a thing but a condition describing the net result of a total effort. You decide what quality means. A canned program to improve quality turns out to be a grab bag of tools, techniques, and slogans, all having their appropriate place and time. Many times the tool is inappropriate, the time is wrong, and quality isn't even the problem. It's the result. For instance, think of the times you go into a store and are disappointed with the result. You don't say to yourself, "Gee, that store needs a quality improvement program." You think in specifics, visualizing that the need for better training, better management, better equipment, better systems, better processing, better whatever. You might say that you were disappointed in the quality, but the return question always asks you to explain your self-referential statement.

THE CUSTOMER IS SELDOM RIGHT

Before we proceed with examining a few specific fad quality improvement programs, like Total Quality Management (TQM) and ISO 9000, we need to return to our claim that the customer is *not* always right. The myth that customers are always right has done more damage than many of the more big-name fads.

Years ago we were fortunate to work with one of the media-proclaimed innovators of Just-in-Time (JIT) inventory management. He was a self-made, American-grown, original business thinker. He became wealthy by challenging conventional thought. What was obvious to most people was perplexing to him; what was obvious to him was downright inaccessible to others. One of the presumptions that perplexed him was that you should run your business as if the customer was always right. He figured since he was in business to provide an industrial product that his customers knew less about than he did, wouldn't it would be natural for his customers to assume that they *didn't* know what they wanted beyond some very vague concepts? If they didn't know the product well enough to build it, how could they always be right? Isn't it more likely that customers are more often wrong than right?

The problem of ignorant customers is familiar to almost everyone in business. It's just impolite to admit it. We find more sales and customer support personnel who disparage their bread-and-butter customers than praise them. The conventional fad fix to this poor attitude is to "educate" your sales and support force so that they better "understand" the customer and are more responsive to his needs. However, if it is painfully obvious that disdain for customers is the rule, not the exception, how successful can a program be when it focuses on the symptom instead of the cause? Quick fixes redefine this systemic conflict as a simple problem of attitude. These programs have to do this in order to construct easily digestible, readily sellable solutions. It's simpler to say that your sales and support people need improvement than to admit your basic business plan needs re-thinking.

Therefore, management fads organized around the customer-is-always-right myth are popular and seemingly successful. For example, in the mid-1990s the Ritz Carlton Hotel Company won the Malcolm Baldrige National

Quality Award in large part because of a proclaimed policy of customer righteousness. Ritz figured that, on average, the customer knows better what he wants than Ritz personnel and by enforcing the core policy of doing everything the customer asked that, on average, they would increase customer satisfaction. Underlying this customer service policy was an assumption that increased customer satisfaction would lead to increased profits. The additional costs to do whatever the customer wants presumably would increase their market share of the very upscale guest market.

Overlooked by casual admirers of the Ritz approach was that for the Ritz many customer requests are billable activities. If a customer asks for his car to be washed and waxed overnight or for a special cuisine, it'll be done, but he'll be appropriately charged. The typical Ritz customer expects to pay for superior service. On the other hand, if a customer doesn't like some part of the service that is considered included in the price of the room, then, of course, making it right is part of the agreed base price. On the other hand, if a customer has all sorts of unusual and expensive requests *and* refuses to pay for them, Ritz will classify that person as a "non-customer." This philosophy—getting the customer what he wants for a price—is not peculiar to the Ritz. They just do it on a bigger, more pricey scale and perhaps are better organized to handle unusual customer requests systematically with a highly trained service staff. The Ritz's actual policy on the ground is not that the customer is always right, but that Ritz employees will do everything they can in order to provide the service they promised to their profile customer. In the rush to emulate the Ritz, the simplifying fad transformation drops half of the equation: the need to identify *exactly* how a policy will make money. Instead, platitudes and obvious-by-inspection attitudes replace well-thought out, quantitative justifications.

This is not a subtle point. The assumption that the customer is always right presupposes you've already defined who your customer is. When this philosophy is put in practice, the second part of the equation is dropped because it's messy. In the real world you cannot separate your customer profile from customer satisfaction and price points. For example, during a recent company function at a fairly expensive Texas steak house, dinner guests were relaxing after the meal. The discussion on one end of the table turned to the meal itself. All were delighted, except one person. She was disappointed, even though she got the exact meal and service the rest of the party did. Asked why she was disappointed, she mentioned she expected more numerous wait staff, better table appointments, and generally a different atmosphere. There was no way that the restaurant could have entertained her disappointments. They design their meal presentation and service around a target customer. She was not their customer even though she thought she was.

That is not to say that the restaurant or any business can ignore a dissatisfied customer. However, your customer service policy *must* be able to differentiate between a complaint from a non-profile customer and one from a profile customer. We'll leave it to you to think about different ways you could construct a system that responds to this difference without aggravating non-customers. Instead, let's spend time underscoring the real trouble you can get into if you don't differentiate. Returning to an industrial sales environment, suppose you make overhead rolling doors and sell them predominately through distributors, who in turn sell them installed to building construction companies. Before you go into business or "reengineer" an old one, you have to define your target distributor. If you don't, your pricing strategy as well as other elements of your business will be disconnected from your cost structure. For instance, if you demand distributors have a high level of product knowledge and installation expertise, you can set your prices lower than if they were moderately familiar with your product. Using knowledgeable distributors lowers your costs by minimizing returns, distributor turn-over, and requests for installation assistance. It also impacts how you run certain parts of your business. For this strategy to work you will have to monitor your customer service department closely to ensure that you can identify and replace distributors who overuse it. Those who overuse are by definition *not* your customers. If you keep them, your costs will begin to rise and your business plan will unravel.

Completing our example, you will eventually face the situation that your kind of distributor does not exist or is not available in every locale. Your choices are to either pick a substandard one and provide specialized training on a planned basis or by-pass that region altogether. You may still call your customer-relations program a "Customer-is-always-Right" derivative, but it is something much different than conventional wisdom. As soon as it looks as if the customer is wrong, your system has to ensure either that you can rehabilitate him or that you drop him as a customer. That's why we say it's better to proclaim a policy of "the customer is seldom right". It takes more thought to understand such a proclamation than it does to swallow an overused and misunderstood myth that customers are always right. Both statements are true, but one reflects the situation better than the other.

This kind of thinking is blasphemous to many of today's management fads that encourage followers to listen to the customer and instill the presumption that the customer is always right. They teach that your customer has all the answers and that he knows better than you about all things related to your product and service. However, to say that you must listen to your customer is not equivalent to saying that the customer is right, even though these two statements are used interchangeably. In reality, as general manager of your company or division, you have to have your own ideas about how you are going to approach a market and how you are going to pick your customers. (Yes, contrary to conventional wisdom, customers don't pick vendors, vendors pick customers.)

TOTAL QUALITY MANAGEMENT (TQM)

Among the countless quality improvement programs making the rounds in the 1980s-1990s, Total Quality Management (TQM) was by far the most durable. Starting out from humble beginnings in the inspection department, its first incarnation was as Total Quality Control (TQC), which gain some level of wide spread acceptance from Dr. Armand V. Feigenbaum's 1961 classical book of the same name. But quality practitioners had bigger plans for themselves. TQC seldom reached into the general management ranks, and without this backing it would never become the self-promotion vehicle that quality control professionals needed. As the quality function became more professionally organized, the old moniker of "control" didn't seem to fit its promise or direction of emerging fad management programs.

The origination of the term ***Total Quality Management*** is debated by people who argue those types of things, but nonetheless it satisfied two constituencies. Quality professionals continued to be disappointed at the limits of their influence and recognized that to improve the reject rates they were experiencing in their inspection departments they would have to expand their reach and authority into other parts of the company. Regardless of the professional politics involved, they were right. The general consensus expressed in the literature of the day pointed out that *control* was an out-of-favor term and really what was needed was general management involvement in the quality function. But a funny thing happened. The trend has not been for more management involvement in the quality function, but more quality function involvement in general management. The vehicle has been TQM.

We've been referring to quality fads such as TQC and TQM without defining them. That is not an oversight, but we figure that if quality practitioners don't have a unified definition of TQM, we don't need one ourselves. A specialized publishing industry surrounds TQM, and depending on the current fad, TQM can take on various forms, permutations, and specialties. Like the word "quality", TQM can mean just about whatever you want. Some of its incarnations include:

- ***Total Quality Control***
  The granddaddy of them all, Total Quality Control (TQC) fell out of favor before it had a chance to be really big. An idea ahead of its time, it was replaced in the collective industrial mind by new, improved versions. In the 1990s Dr. Feigenbaum's book (mentioned above) was in its third edition and still in print. It is an excellent reference for the practice of quality control and is extremely readable and practical for a technical book aimed at engineers. It identifies the practice of quality control as it applies throughout the production cycle, from product development to delivery, thus the inclusion of the word "total" in the title. Dr. Feigenbaum unified these distributed functions under this one function called quality, but implied that the tools he recounts were for everyone, not just the "quality staff." The Doctor's one shortcoming, if he had any, seems to have been his lack of effective self-promotion.

- ***The Deming Method***
For many, TQM is embodied in the teachings of Dr. W. Edwards Deming, although Dr. Deming never, as far as we know, identified his methods with the TQM tag. His name appears on the Deming Prize, a national quality award presented in Japan by a quasi-governmental bureaucracy charged with "guiding" industrial development in Japan. Deming became a quality guru in America when the press decided that everything American was inferior and everything Japanese superior. The American media's early 1980s investigation of this crisis turned up Dr. Deming. They proclaimed him as standing at the headwaters of the impressive, authentic improvement of Japanese products. (It seems convenient that American journalists found the savior of Japanese industry to be an American.) While in some ways Dr. Deming did play an important role in the Japanese industrial transformation, the situation was and continues to be more complicated than that. Nevertheless, the management fad industry found a new product in Dr. Deming's tools, techniques, and philosophy. His widely-repeated association with Ford's quality improvement initiatives ensured a steady market for books written by others explaining Dr. Deming's somewhat eclectic collection of principles, called "Deming's Fourteen Points." An entire industry of consultants, working day and night, dissected and re-packaged Dr. Deming's prognostications for quality improvement. He had two basic, but not new, messages. First, he emphasized that "quality" was the responsibility, if not the sole reason for the existence, of general management. He was continually disappointed that his audiences were pre-

dominately populated by middle managers since he knew that change would only come if the leaders of industry got religion. Second, his approach to product improvement was process-oriented. He seemingly single-handedly re-introduced statistical process control to American manufacturers, de-emphasizing inspection as the cornerstone of nonconformance avoidance. He came down from the mountain to remind us that "you can't inspect quality into a product." Once people started listening to him he had many other things to say, and wound up settling on his famous Fourteen Points.

- ***Statistical Process Control***
  Dr. Deming's black bag was statistical process control (SPC). The predominate tool of his form of industrial medicine was the control chart, a statistical method for analyzing the output of a process to determine the inherent capability of the process. From such analysis, the production staff was supposed to identify special causes of production upsets and management was supposed to identify the opportunity for improving the entire process through investment in better tools, technology, and training. For some people, SPC and TQM became synonymous since the rest of Dr. Deming's teachings were more difficult to transform into a quick-fix. Fifteen years after the Big Bang of the American Quality Universe, several well-known and respectable consulting firms continue to be organized around such a limited TQM toolbox and do quite well.

- ***The Juran Institute***
  Dr. Joseph M. Juran was a contemporary of Dr. Deming's and participated in the early efforts to help Japanese industry recover from the destruction of World War II. The professional relationship between these two proclaimed pioneers has been variously described as "friendly" to "cordial" to "cool" to "envious" to "hostile." The truth is unavailable to us and (according to decision analysis) most likely something entirely different and immaterial. The reality is that while both men had interesting things to say about quality control and the role of management, Deming's ideas were the first to be converted into a wide-spread industrial-cultural phenomena by the American management fad machine, and to the first mover go the spoils. While Dr. Juran has written many books on quality, his *Quality Control Handbook*, which first appeared in 1951, remains his most popular contribution to the practice and is considered by some to be the bible on the subject. Not as well written as Dr. Feigenbaum's *Total Quality Control*, it nonetheless seems to include every quality control subject in the world (literally), ensuring a wide market and making it a very thick and heavy book that every self-respecting quality manager should have.

- ***The Crosby School***
  Philip Crosby was the right man in the right place at the right time. His book, *Quality is Free*, published in 1979, appeared at the same time the popular press discovered Dr. Deming. He wrote other books on various topics, including *The Art of Getting Your Own Sweet Way*, *Running Things*, and *The Eternally Successful Organization*. Mr.

Crosby's talent was marketing his ideas through an adult education company called Crosby Associates, Inc. For a time, it seemed that every up-and-coming middle manager in America was sent to Crosby's Florida campus to be inculcated with Phil's philosophy. Serious gurus with "Dr." in front of their name didn't think much of his sloganeering and rah-rah approach to quality, but the market sure did. While he, too, had a hodgepodge of points to present, we mostly associate the re-invigorization of "cost of quality" and the slogan Zero Defects to his camp. Mis-named, the cost of quality really should have been called "the cost of non-conformance." Crosby also realized that the emerging quality profession would get nowhere fast unless it talked the language of general management. He set about teaching quality professionals and upper-management wanna-bes established methods for quantifying how much rework and nonconforming product cost business so that they could return to their jobs and get the message across to the people who really made the decisions. Instead of trying to reform general management as Deming was attempting, Crosby went about re-educating middle management. Because of his approach, Crosby was a big proponent of defining quality as conformance to specification, and for that he was metaphorically crucified by quality purists who spent their free time arguing about the "real" meaning of quality. Like many quick-fix quality initiatives, Crosby's methods had little new to say, but they used refreshing narrative and had an easy style that sold well.

- ***National Quality Awards***
  Not to be outdone by Japanese bureaucrats, the U.S. federal bureaucracy, with the support of various large U.S. companies and quality-profession organizations, came up with their own measure of excellence, the Malcolm Baldrige National Quality Award. It is awarded every year to fewer than a handful of companies competing in categories that group them by size and nature of business. The Baldrige award has had its good years and its bad. Some were astonished the year the Cadillac division of General Motors won the award since other measures of conformance and reliability did not put Cadillac anywhere near the top. Another year the award was presented to a company that went bankrupt shortly afterward. Nevertheless, the appearance of a national quality award provided a forum (and government money) for quality professionals to thrash out the exact meaning of TQM. Not only is this effort slow going, an overlapping international effort to define TQM was underway at the time this book went to press (1995). This group began their epic struggle by trying to define the difference between quality assurance and quality management and promptly bogged down. Presumably, they skipped the definition of quality since they convinced themselves that they had a handle on it. We doubt it.

All the thunder and noise about TQM drowns out the genuine moaning of real people frustrated by their management's failure to attend to its responsibilities. Deming was right. The care and feeding of the operating system is the sole business of general management. When that responsibility is parcelled out to functions unable to influence behavior across the board, middle managers become prematurely grey. It doesn't take long for these trapped animals to realize that a TQM program of whatever flavor is the preferred (although temporary) escape route, compared to fighting their way out by telling the boss he's not doing his job. Aside from systemic problems caused by undefinable terms and unmeasurable criteria, TQM programs continue to fail because general management is not convinced real change is necessary, and if it is, they are not convinced that the change starts and ends with them.

INTERNATIONAL HOUSE OF PANCAKES IS A CONSPIRACY

In the late 1980s and throughout the 1990s, American business was nearly overwhelmed by something broadly called "ISO 9000." This was a code word for inviting an independent third-party assessor to examine objective evidence at your facility and then certify that the documented "quality assurance program" met the requirements of one of a series of international standards, collectively called ISO 9000. Uninformed journalists and instant consultants ran three-column high headlines uncovering all sorts of European conspiracies (the governing body of ISO was in Geneva, Switzerland), ISO-based export requirements and restrictions, and vendor mandates for certification. The fact that certification was a commercial activity, wholly and independently separate from the quality standards themselves, didn't prevent the management fad industry from using fear to promote the newest wave of "you-got-to-do-this-or-you-won't-be-a-player" mania.

The real disaster with the ISO certification fad was that the value of the quality systems standards themselves was totally obliterated by commercial certification drumbeat. More to the point, the certification game actually had a negative value for American industry and unfortunately was entropic—once industry started down this path, it had no way to come back to the starting point. Quality systems certification eventually will resemble other various product certification programs familiar to industries that build quasi-regulated products. It will be susceptible to conflicts-of-interest, double-dealing, pay-offs, fraud, and general bad-guy type stuff. Customers will demand their vendors have third-parties certification of their quality systems, but the process will add nothing but cost. This sad outcome is not in question. We have plenty of industrial history and human nature guaranteeing it.

Buried somewhere under this avalanche of ISO 9000 commercialization lies the real value of operating system standards. Disregarding that quality may appear in their names, operating standards outline systematic approaches to organizing your business. Of course, anything you do to improve the operation of your company impacts quality. In many cases these standards can be traced to efforts organized by quality practitioners who attempted to define qualitative issues in terms of quantifiable, observable actions. They are helpful guides in their original form. As they become requirements subject to outside interpretation, they lose all their intellectual authority and become someone else's property. These standards go by various names (e.g., quality assurance standards, quality management standards, good manufacturing practices) and are available from various sources (e.g., industrial associations, professional societies, large buying cooperatives). They can embody good, vetted ideas about generic operating systems, but as quality professionals seek to expand their industrial influence during the various revision cycles, groupthink will rule. For example, national quality awards had their beginnings in generic operating standards and are a good source of operation system design ideas. However, during the mid-1990s they began to include more politically-correct but immaterial directives concerning employee empowerment and organizational design. This creeping tendency to take basic, generic models and modify them to include "accepted" models of corporate behavior means that a good grounding in the six fundamental management principles presented in this book is necessary to avoid swallowing some of their more contrived elements.

CULTURE CLUB

Given the problems and considerable effort required to implement well-defined operational changes, imagine the kinds of problems associated with grandiose schemes to change a company's "culture." Applying the fundamentals we've presented, how does a cultural change project stack up? Poorly, that's how. First, if you thought defining quality was difficult, try defining culture. Second, suppose we pretend that you can generate a reasonable definition of culture. How are you going to measure your progress towards transforming the culture you have into the culture you want? How will you know when you've arrived? How do you know for certain that the new culture is "better" than the old?

Most of what passes for culture is really cultural artifacts. Just as it is difficult to draw inferences from archaeological artifacts, it is almost impossible to say something intelligent about a company's culture by looking at its artifacts. These are immensely difficult problems that trip up people trained in the science of sociology and anthropology all the time. They have raging debates about culture and its effects on those residing in it. Any fad management initiative claiming to change company culture is a fraud. It can't be done, shouldn't be done, and mustn't be done. Culture, like quality, is what you have after the day is done. It's not something you can manipulate, manage, forecast, and change. The time you waste pretending that you are improving your culture could be better put to use improving your product, understanding your market, or enjoying a day at the beach. Speculating on how to change your culture is a non-starter unless you're talking about changing companies.

MY BENCHMARK WON'T RETURN MY PHONE CALLS

The problem with benchmarking is two-fold. The methodology is internally inconsistent, and if that's not enough to bury it, it assumes that the past is prologue. The past is prologue if we're talking about the sweep of history; it's nearly irrelevant on the level of company operations.

Initially, benchmarking appealed to companies at the bottom of the heap because it supposedly pointed a path to the top. But what if you're at the top? Benchmarking doesn't help you. In fact, the success of benchmarking depends on getting good information about competitors or, in the absence of competitors, trying to find "similar" industries to benchmark against. Since companies at the top of their market have little competitive incentive to share their true competitive advantages, benchmarking databases could become dangerously skewed. People selling benchmarking information try to overcome this problem by appealing to the vanity of market leaders. They convinced some of these leaders that benchmarking information could be helpful in determining how far ahead the leaders were. Nothing like patting yourself on the back.

But wait. If benchmarking isn't such a bonanza for the guys on top, why should it be good for guys on the bottom? The essence of benchmarking is that you should copy the practices of the best. If the best don't benchmark, should you? As soon as you show that benchmarking is not so good for one segment, the whole intellectual premise supporting it collapses.

Suppose that this fatal flaw didn't exist. Let's try another. Why should you follow a fad that focuses on the past if the consensus is that you should focus on the future? (Okay, we're relying on consensus thinking, which we've pretty much said is unreliable, but then we're only having fun here. We've already proven that benchmarking is a worthless science.) For example, in 1996 Ford introduced an entirely reengineered Taurus based on the direction that Ford thought Toyota was taking their Camry. Surprise! While Ford was chasing Toyota (in essence benchmarking against the Camry), Toyota went the other way. The 1997 Camry was scheduled to move toward fewer options and lower cost while the Taurus was becoming more feature laden and more expensive. Time will tell which strategy paid off, but if Ford succeeds it won't be for its forward-thinking planning, nor will it prove benchmarking's worth. After all, perfect benchmarking, in which time lags do not play a factor, would have resulted in Ford moving down the features and price curve, not up. The impotence of benchmarking is obvious to any rational thinker, but as a fad it replaces thinking with fashion.

EPILOGUE

While these discussions may have seemed a wee bit sharp, they have to be. Our point is not that these fads don't have value; it is that their value can be buried so deep during their conversion to fad status that their value becomes all but obscure. Much of the problem is rooted in the absence of critical analysis by managers who lack a grounding in fundamental management skills.

Our list of management fads is heavily weighted with quality-based fads because at the time of the first edition of this book quality was King of the Fads. It wasn't always that way; every generation born during the Era of the Fad has its favorite path to quick riches and glory. When this book is updated a few years from now, only the names will change; the impotence of fad management movements will remain.

16

Chapter 16

The Redemption

For our last bit of irreverence, we'd like to discuss endings. Many of today's popular management initiatives conclude by saying that they never end. We are supposed to believe that their wisdom is so profound and their tools so powerful that your life will be influenced forever. That may be true. A management program initiated at the right time can have disproportional impact on some people. However, the reality for most of us is that management programs do end, usually by being replaced by yet another program, and that is not necessarily bad. The assumption that a change program is never ending because change is never ending does a gross injustice to the reality of change dynamics. The nature of any program is that it *must* reach closure for participants to feel a sense of accomplishment. Otherwise, no one can build on past experience. *Change requires closure.*

While some fad management programs don't provide closure because they don't understand the basic elements of change, others avoid discussing closure because they can't imagine what would replace them, and therefore they can't come to grips with the final chapter. We can. We want you to think about the six fundamental skills. Can you list them aloud without referring to Chapter 3? If you can't, you're fairly average, and therein lies the point of our book. The difference between successful managers and mediocre ones is that the successful ones recognize their limitations and fashion their *own* program to do something about them. Sure, you might hire a consultant to help build a proprietary program, but the program is yours. It will have a starting point, a middle, and a defined end. The fundamental skills for identifying the valuable elements of your program and for setting profitable objectives are here in this book anytime you want to re-visit them.

As you try your very own improvement project on yourself, you probably will emphasize one fundamental over another. After all, you can't work on every facet of your skill set every single day. You have to take a break once in a while; you have to get closure on your latest efforts; and you have to re-visit some of your earlier failures to get inspiration for your next move. We wish you the best of luck. We know how hard real change is.

Before we go, we'd like to leave you with a view larger than just business management by showing that the management profession is far from the only occupation susceptible to faddish behavior. During the mid-1990s psychology suffered through another one of its periodic molts. The public feasted on stories of psychiatric patients recounting satanic ritual abuse with the help of certified therapists using hypnotic techniques said to uncover repressed childhood memories. The number of cases uncovered could only be explained by assuming the existence of a wide-spread, organized satanic conspiracy in America. Despite the fact that no one could produce physical evidence showing that these cults ever existed, the practice of using elicited repressed memories for diagnosis became accepted treatment in clinics that were organized specifically for treatment of this new mental disorder. Repressed memory therapy, especially that which uncovered heretofore repressed episodes of long-term sexual abuse, became the profession's newest fad. Like fads of all persuasions, this one hitched a ride on the back of orthodox practice. Legitimate cases of memory repression were documented, and success rates were sufficient to allow its illegitimate application by questionable practitioners.

The common thread between medical treatment fads and business fads is how fringe practices become mainstream. The profession makes a small home for it in the name of tolerance and curiosity, only to find that with time it claims wide-spread acceptance. Recognizing that fads are not unique to business brings some comfort, but not enough when we consider the damage they do to the economy as a whole. Moreover, on a personal level, they can be devastating, and not just because people lose jobs when their company wastes precious time fiddling with fads instead of working on its problems. Even if a company doesn't fail and put people out of work, the psychic damage is considerable. A career peppered with meaningless work driven by a never ending parade of business fads is a poor portrait for reflection during your twilight years.

We know that many people are overwhelmed by the faddish behavior surrounding them. It's hard, if not impossible, to run the opposite direction of a mob. People have lost their lives resisting the rush of a panicked crowd. If you felt that way before reading this book, we hope it gave you the tools to dig out of this avalanche or at least gave you enough air so that you can hold out for the rescue team. If you find yourself in a management team shot full of fad fever, your time will come between the fading of the current fad and the blossoming of another. This cycle is inevitable, and the lull seems to come once every two to three years, so it won't be long. In the meantime you have to shore up your own intellectual foundations so that when sufficient disconfirming information is available, you can use it to encourage real discussion about change, improvement, and profit.

Appendix

This bibliography is arranged by subject.

CHANGE DYNAMICS

Beckhard, Richard & Harris, Reuben T. *Organizational Transitions: Managing Complex Change (Second Edition).* Reading, MA: Addison-Wesley, 1987.

A pamphlet-sized book that is surprisingly complete; for those who feel more comfortable cooking with a recipe.

Schein, Edgar H. *Planning and Managing Change.* MIT Management in the 1990s Research Program Working Paper (#90s: 88-056). Boston: MIT Sloan School of Management, October 1988.

The authors' original source of ideas about the stages of the change process.

DECISION THEORY

Dawes, Robyn M. *Rational Choice in an Uncertain World.* San Diego: Harcourt Brace Jovanovich, 1988.

Heavy into the probabilistic nature of uncertain outcomes; an excellent treatment of the subject but requires concentrated effort to get the most from it.

Hogarth, Robin. *Judgement and Choice: The Psychology of Decision (Second Ed.).* Chichester, Great Britain, 1987.

Overlaps Dawes somewhat, but concentrates more on cognitive limitations. If you don't understand Dawes, try Hogarth or visa versa.

Janis, Irving L. *Groupthink: Psychological Studies of Policy Decisions and Fiascoes.* Boston: Houghton Mifflin, 1982.

A great read if you like inside stories of power, politics, and influential people screwing up because they're full of themselves.

DECISION-MAKING TOOLS

Behn, Robert D., & Vaupel, James W. *Quick Analysis for Busy Decision Makers.* New York: Basic Books, Inc., 1982.

Well-written "how-to" book about decision analysis, especially decision trees.

FADS

Each of these books was the basis for the management fad it started. They are shown here because we refer to them elsewhere in the book. Dr. Deming's style is a bit hard to read. You might try The Deming Management Method *by Mary Walton (New York: Putnam, 1986) for an easier read.*

Covey, Stephen R. *The Seven Habits of Highly Effective People: Powerful Lessons in Personal Change.* New York: Simon & Schuster, 1989. [Also published with the subtitle of "Restoring the Character Ethic"]

Crosby, Philip B. *Quality Is Free: The Art of Making Quality Certain.* New York: McGraw-Hill, 1979.

Deming, Edwards W. *Out of the Crisis.* Cambridge, MA: MIT Center for Advanced Engineering Study, 1986.

Hammer, Michael, & Champy, James. *Reengineering the Corporation: A Manifesto for Business Revolution.* New York: HarperCollins, 1993

GESTALT CYCLE OF EXPERIENCE

Nevis, Edwin C. *Organizational Consulting: A Gestalt Approach.* New York: Gardner Press, Inc., 1987.

Primarily written for process consultants, this book has a wealth of good ideas for general managers, including a detailed explanation of the Gestalt cycle.

MEETINGS

Jay, Antony. How to run a meeting. *Harvard Business Review,* March–April 1976.

Good advice is never dated. Still the best treatment of the subject.

QUALITY AS A FUNCTION

These two books describe nearly all elements of the practice of the quality control.

Feignenbaum, Armand V. Total Quality Control (Third Edition). New York: McGraw-Hill, 1991.

Juran, J.M. (Editor-in-Chief). *Juran's Quality Control Handbook (Fourth Edition).* New York: McGraw-Hill, 1988.

SELF-REFERENTIALISM

Guillen, Michael. *Bridges to Infinity: The Human Side of Mathematics.* Los Angeles: Jeremy P Tarcher, Inc., 1983.

A great bedtime reader (really). Short, well-written chapters on profound mathematical and philosophical problems; accessible to anyone faintly curious about mathematics, physics and the universe. Good treatment of Gödel's Incompleteness Theorem, but no mention of quality.

Index

The page numbers shown refer to the beginning of the primary passage for the referenced subject.

About the Authors

KENNETH DURHAM

Mr. Durham graduated with honors from the University of Texas where he earned a BS in electrical engineering and has an MBA from the MIT Sloan School of Management. He was a co-founder of Quality International LLP, and is a principal with the Quantum Institute, which is profiled on the next page. He has held chief operating officer and technical management positions in *Fortune 500* companies as well as start-ups. His assignments have included work ranging from mineral extraction to high-alloy metalworking to low-tech manufacturing to pure service. He has authored a wide range of titles including peer-reviewed engineering dissertations as well as general business topics.

BRUCE KENNEDY

Mr. Kennedy graduated from the University of Central Oklahoma with a BA in marketing. He is the president of the Quantum Institute. He has held management positions in several *Fortune 500* companies and was a founding partner in three successful start-up companies. He is a recognized authority in vendor relations, inventory management, logistics, and the use of standards-based management systems. He has addressed over 40 professional organizations and held related seminars in over 60 leading corporations during the past three years. His writings about management issues have been published throughout the U.S. and Europe by numerous technical institutions, universities, trade organizations, and professional societies.

About the Quantum Institute

The **Quantum Institute** is an executive training, publishing, and process consulting firm that specializes in helping business owners and key corporate officers meet their profit objectives by developing core leadership skills and process insight. The Institute was formed as a result of work with a proprietary list of American corporate leaders engaged in various change initiatives. The successful methods and concepts associated with those efforts led to the *Maze Series,* a collection of treatises concerning American business leadership at the end of the 20th century, of which *Escaping the Maze* is the premier public-domain publication.

For more information concerning the Institute, call

(713) 690-0305.